SCIENCE AND TRUTH

Betty Sue Bryan
2001

SCIENCE AND TRUTH

By

L. ALLEN HIGLEY, Ph. D., D. Sc.

Revised and Edited by
BETTY SUE BRYAN, M.A.

ISBN: 0-75960-401-0

This book is printed on acid free paper.

1stBooks - rev. 01/11/01

ACKNOWLEDGEMENTS

Wayne D. Bryan, Th.D., Hebrew Old Testament.

John May, Ph.D., Chair of English Department at Louisiana State University 1992.

Daniel P. Higley, for his good will and prayers on behalf of this undertaking of his father's book and to his wife, Marge, for her help.

For the science classes at LSU which I enjoyed and from which I learned a great deal.

Professors Gloria and Lawrence Sasek, English Department, Louisiana State University; and to Rev. Tommy French, pastor of Jefferson Baptist Church, Baton Rouge, Louisiana for their constant encouragement of this work.

TABLE OF CONTENTS

ABOUT THE AUTHOR

L. Allen Higley

Born in 1871 in Wilmot, Ohio. Died 1955 in Bridgeport, Connecticut. Taught Chemistry and Geology at: Wheaton College in Wheaton, IL, 1925-1939; at the King's College in Belmar, NJ (later relocated in New Castle, DE), 1939-1950.

Was the New Mexico State Chemist,1919-1920s, as well as Consulting Geologist for oil in New Mexico and Texas.

Received Doctor of Philosophy in Organic Chemistry from the University of Chicago in 1907; later the honorary Doctor of Science degree from Ohio Northern University, Ada, OH, where he had previously earned his Bachelor of Science degree.

In the 1940s, he contributed a third of all the geological specimens at the Chicago Field Museum.

Dr. Higley shows that there is actually no conflict between real science and Biblical truth, that there is no basis in fact for the evolutionary theory of creation, and that Biblical statements can be verified.

He brings Science and Mathematics to bear on his proof, and he makes the fact of creation according to the Genesis account so clear that the layman cannot fail to follow his reasoning.

The work will be invaluable assistance to those whom the Bible is a closed book because of its supposed internal conflict and its alleged conflict with "real" science.

I

THE TRUE FOUNDATION

Discoveries in science have become so numerous that they no longer surprise us; they have become so extensive that they prove bewildering. As a result, facts have not been classified adequately or correlated fully. Science has sought to find the explanation for its basic problems in purely secular and scientific fields. But these explanations are too widely at variance to be satisfactory. They appear right to some and correspondingly wrong to others. Such attempts as these are in reality mere speculations. They can have no lasting place in science, because true science is concerned with facts and with abiding truth.

Science in itself cannot possibly meet its own basic problems, so we must turn to something other than the scientific and secular. There is one remaining source of help. Its authority has been fully tested and never found wanting—the Bible. All true science finally rests on this one foundation. It is the book of ultimate origins. This science will endure because there can be no true science without this foundation. Already the decline of false science is evident. The increasing conflicts between nations are being fought out by wars conceded to be the most scientific of all time. They are also increasing in frequency and horror.

Most recently, science in the field of astronomy has had to revise, correct, and update its thinking because of the discoveries the new giant Hubble Space Telescope is making. This high precision instrument, revolving 370 miles above us, with it 94.6 inch primary mirror, can show phenomena of the universe in much greater detail and at much greater distances than ever

1

before imagined.[1] Large galaxies of stars in such vast numbers have appeared that some previous assumptions prove to be woefully lacking.

In the field of biochemistry, the discovery of the double helix structure of the DNA and complex proteins can lead to finding cures for sickle cell anemia, opening up the possibility of fetal surgery, and so forth.

The discovery of plate tectonics in the field of geology explains the movements and deformation of the earth's crust on a large scale. Formation of mountains, continental drift, earthquakes are now more clearly understood.

These are just a few examples of the great explosion of information and discoveries made in the last four decades. No doubt more surprises are ahead, and we all look forward to them.

Multitudes of people have been told that the Bible is a myth. They accept this view without consideration. Disregard for the Bible has become so common, especially among the educated class, that many people think it a mark of enlightenment to hold the Bible in disrepute. "The wisdom of this world is foolishness with God. For it is written, He taketh the wise in their own craftiness." (I. Corinthians 3:19.) "Keep that which is committed to thy trust, avoiding profane and vain babblings, and oppositions of science falsely so called." (I. Timothy 6:20.)

Through indifference and the neglect of its reading, many are robbing themselves of their greatest privilege. The fact still remains that it is the most widely circulated of all books, and it has been translated into more languages than any other book. Men and women have lived and died by it and for it. Many have testified to its elevating power.

The Bible has supplied the dominant and highest theme for the greatest and most enduring of the arts: paintings, sculpture, poetry, prose, music. The facts prove that the Bible is the

---

[1] Valerie Neal, Exploring the Universe with the Hubble Space Telescope (Washington, D.C.: NASA, 1990).

2

priceless treasure of all ages. We disregard it at our own peril. Instead of setting it aside, let us learn how to use it.

We will regard it the same way we would any other book from which we hope to benefit. We must at least be reasonable. In mathematics, for example, we expect to be governed by the law of numbers if we wish to understand and learn how to use them. Likewise the Bible, also of final authority, must be understood and used on its own terms. These terms are always consistent, hence possible. Our own terms are not so since man is fallible.

Righteousness and justice are the terms. Sin is spoken of so that it can be done away with and righteousness may take its place. We are given the plan of redemption from sin so that we may avail ourselves of the offer. The terms are always reasonable. They were devised by the Creator who alone has the power and wisdom to enforce them.

A very common mistake is to listen to the wrong authority on the Bible, such as those who are authorities in some field of secular learning which leaves God out of consideration. Mere secular authority does not qualify someone to pass judgement on something as sacred as the Bible. One who has always been blind cannot be an authority on light. Our first parents, Adam and Eve, were misled by following this kind of authority.

Modern higher education is largely under its influence and as a result is working great harm. Perhaps this is the reason so many of our young people in America are not going into the field of Science. So much that is being forced on them in many schools contradicts some previous Christian teaching, or influence, and they find it impossible to reconcile these conflicts.

Another mistake would be to draw a general conclusion on an isolated statement or a single quotation from the Bible. We must consider the context, else we become hasty and careless readers. Conclusions come quickly rather than accurately. We wouldn't do this with explosives because there is too much at stake. Too many decide on their own what they will accept as truth and reject as false, accepting something not fully established or rejecting what they know to be truth. This is subjective reading. They have personal biases and limitations. They are governed by environment and a habit of thinking which glorifies man. God's loving patience is mistaken for disinterest or lack of power. Disregard for God's word leads to rebellion against Him. This is the greatest sin of our time.

The Bible differs from all other books. It must be read in a different manner. What we think of it is of little importance. What does God think of us? We must read it objectively, with the prayer that God will show us how to read it. We have to be wholly surrendered to His will. His glory, and that which honors Him the most, will result in our giving Him the benefit of the doubt. Real truth should then be found sooner or later.

Reading the Bible is doing something separate from and above ourselves, like the difference between that which is holy and that which is sinful. We are debtors in every respect. Reading the Bible leads to <u>eternal</u> good versus <u>temporal</u> good. Eternal good is the priceless gift of God. Temporal good is the snare of the world.

In considering two statements in the Bible which seem to be contradictory, accept both statements as true. Find the explanation in the context. Both may be true at different times or under different circumstances. This is a cardinal rule: an obscure passage never contradicts a clear passage. Don't read the Bible as if blinded to the rule of common sense, or you will fail to recognize the inspiration and accuracy of the Bible. Those who do read the Bible sujectively accept the statement most preferred and adhere to it at the expense of the other. This is always wrong. It makes the Bible confusing just as it would any other book.

In the original language it is the inspired word of God. The Old Testament was written in Hebrew. The New Testament was written in Greek and Aramaic, the latter being the language of the times when Jesus spoke. Translations may contain some errors. The Bible is absolute truth, not subject to change by any mere human agency. If accepted step by step, it will be

4

understood. We must observe the rule that what is not yet understood is fully as true as that which is already understood. This is not merely an intellectual matter. It is a spiritual matter, requiring repentance of sin, acceptance of God for full salvation, and obedience to His word. Who would expect to understand the science of engineering without submitting to its laws?

In science no investigation of personal sin is required for further work. In the Bible there is. When facts of science are standardized Biblically, their classification becomes simplified. All phenomena of the natural world have an adequate and definite objective. Life loses its meaningless mystery and becomes a sublime miracle. Bewildering facts become understandable.

II

SOME ESSENTIAL PRINCIPLES OF CREATION

The world was created according to immutable Law, which must be understood if we would comprehend creation. "It is the glory of God to conceal a thing." (Proverbs 25:2.) "O the depth of the riches both of the wisdom and knowledge of God!" (Romans 11:33.) "The secret things belong unto the Lord our God." (Deut. 29:29.)

We may glorify God in seeking principles of creation which are plainly implied in the Bible:

The Principle of Law and Obedience

God created two orders of moral beings with free will. They were created as free moral agents and rulers. The first of such beings were the angels. After they failed as rulers of the earth, God created man to take their place. Both orders of beings were created with certain needs, which were supplied by the physical world which had previously been created to supply such needs.

The system of creation required coordination. It seems highly complex when seen from the human standpoint. It could function perfectly only when fully coordinated. This always necessitates law. Such laws are inherent by virtue of creation in the physical and biological world. Hence there was no possibility of failure in the physical world and in plant and animal life. The coordination was perfect by virtue of its creation.

When this system was placed under the rulership of a creation endowed with free will, a new condition arose in the world unlike the previous one when free will did not exist. No

6

ruler created to rule in God's place is fit to rule over anything unless he is bound by the same laws of order as the Creator Himself. The free will of the creature, like that of the Creator, is limited by the laws of the system. Else confusion and destruction enter into the world. The creature is not free to violate these laws without suffering the penalty.

The perfect functioning of that part of the world which had no free will was necessarily dependent upon the perfect functioning of its ruler who had free will. The former was created for the pleasure of the latter. Perfect pleasure must be conditioned upon a corresponding obedience to the laws involved.

Those free will beings created to rule in God's place were aware of that which was required of them for their own safety and that of the whole system. As long as they functioned perfectly under the law of perfect obedience, their needs would be supplied perfectly and perpetually. The world would not decline and run down through loss of energy.

The food supply would be perpetual also. Obedience is keeping the revealed law, but breaking the law is sin.

When the being possessing free will chose to disobey, it brought disruption into the whole system involved. Such a condition of necessity terminated both the system and the life of the being that caused the disorder even though the being was a ruler. His disobedience proved his unworthiness and incapacity to rule. It was better for him to die than to continue under conditions which were out of harmony with the plan of creation.

However, God does not permit this destruction to go on to its climax. His great love had already provided a plan to save man from the consequences of sin. The final end will the "new heavens and a new earth, wherein dwelleth righteousness." (11Peter 3:13.) Then there will be perfect obedience to divine law everywhere. God's servants will then serve Him. (Rev. 22:3.) The system will be perpetual because it will be free from sin and disobedience. Had man never disobeyed, he would never have known suffering. Nevertheless, he may still find perfection for himself, if he follows God's plan for attaining it.

Some one may wish to inquire as to what will be done with the fallen angels. The Bible does not reveal this to us, because the Bible gives God's plan of redemption for man, not for angels. If there is one for them, it is not a matter of man's concern, for it does not involve man. Angels are mentioned only in so far as they are involved in man's welfare. Man's first sin was influenced by a fallen angel; man under sin is sometimes ministered to by sinless angels. These are therefore mentioned.

The principles involved in creation are a part of God's eternal plan. They were necessary in the beginning and have remained necessary ever since. There are few who are willing to concede to God as Creator of the world the rights and duties that they would concede to the head of, let's say, a railroad system. Yet the Creator's rights are infinitely greater. He is the absolute owner of everything in His own right. Abram called Him "the most high God, the possessor of heaven and earth." (Genesis 14:22.) This must be true because He brought it into being out of nothing. (Gen. 1:1.) There was no preexisting material that belonged to another being (bara – to create out of nothing).

He has the right to insist on obedience. It is not only His right, but it is also His duty because of His love for His creatures. He must protect them from evil; thus He must protect His system of creation from the disobedient, from the thief who would rob and destroy.

People understand these principles readily when applied to practical affairs like property rights. But when applied to moral and spiritual relations between man and man, or man and God, the great majority pretend not to see their duty. The Ten Commandments are called old-fashioned; we have "outgrown" them in the twentieth century.

Since murder and theft were wrong at one time, we ask upon what grounds these sins can be justified as right at the present time? No one has ever shown how the sin of one time may become the virtue of another time. A law of the state does not always involve matters of permanent right and wrong, because it is based upon changing human standards.

The violation of God's laws, without penalty, makes for an impossible world for the very ones who would claim to benefit from it the most. These commands involve matters of eternal justice. God's Word is eternally true. It can never be set aside. Law is the very nature of things. The laws of truth and righteousness are written in the very nature of creation itself. No one can honestly claim otherwise. The murderer may assert that he has the right to take a life, but he is unwilling to concede to others that right, lest he himself be killed.

The Principle of Unquestioning Obedience

God is pleased with unquestioning and full obedience first of all. Human understanding may come later. It need not necessarily come at all. Nothing is fully understood by man anyway. How foolish to delay obedience until one understands. Knowledge of the will of God should be sufficient understanding for any one.

Questioning beyond this implies the spirit of disobedience. It is often the very beginning of the disobedient attitude towards a command and may soon grow into sinful disobedience. If repeated long enough, it tends to lawlessness.

We observe that the child that is trained to unquestioning obedience very soon becomes fully obedient in spirit and is happy in it. If a child is allowed to question the commands given it, and if allowed to continue, this child will soon become very disobedient. A child usually questions first on the ground of not understanding the nature of the command. Gaining concessions by this attitude, it soon goes further and questions the need of the command itself. Soon the child wants the privilege of obeying only at its own pleasure. But no real satisfaction comes from it. The child trained to full obedience finds happiness as its reward. This is the law written in the very nature of creation.

Soldiers, regardless of rank, are trained first of all to unquestioning obedience. Else an early defeat could be invited. In active military work no one would ever think of doing the things that are so commonly tolerated in other walks of life.

Human nature, as regards obedience, was much the same in the Bible times as it is at present. In His early ministry, Christ told His disciples that He would be killed and that on the third day He would rise again. (Matthew 16:21; Luke 24:7.) The disciples knew this and knew also that Jesus expected them to believe it. After it had come to pass, Thomas doubted even after he was told the fact. "Except I shall see in His hands the print of the nails, and put my finger into the print of the nails, and thrust my hand into His side, I will not believe." (John 20:25.) After seeing the risen Christ, he was later to say, "My Lord and my God." (John 20:28.) Jesus commanded him not to be "faithless, but believing." Then Jesus said to him, "Thomas, because thou hast seen me, thou has believed: blessed are they that have not seen, and yet have believed." (John 20:29.)

Thus, on the authority of Jesus Himself, a blessing is pronounced upon those who believe without seeing. He did not pronounce a blessing upon Thomas for believing only after he had seen. (John 20:29.)

The spirit of complete obedience is what we all lack. Our first parents failed in it. They were commanded plainly not to eat the forbidden fruit, but they disobeyed. (Gen. 2:17, 3:6.) We have all followed in the same course. Jesus was the one man of perfect obedience. This was evidence that He is also sinless. We are not God. When we acknowledge our sin of disobedience, He is faithful to forgive us. But most people are too proud to admit their sin. Thus sin is heaped upon sin, and general lawlessness prevails. It is the common failure of our time.

Impenitent sinners have one trait in common. They will not concede to others the right to do what they themselves do. That might interfere with their own plans of sin. Recently, by way of example, some "artists" have wanted to yell "foul" when those

10

with a moral and ethical conscience sought legislation passed that would deny them grants from the National Endowment for the Arts. They felt freedom of expression should have no restrictions even if it meant depicting scenes desecrating the cross of Christ and other things sacred.

Yet when those offended wished to withdraw their money for the subsidizing of such "art", these same offenders did not wish to be told that their depraved scenes and their obscenity were not subject matter for prurient charges. Such people wish to judge and ridicule others, but they do not wish to be held in contempt themselves. No one who is honest with himself and God will ever be deceived.

The most that can be said in favor of the sinner is that he is not responsible for the sin that was in the world when he was born, nor for any of the sinful environment around him before he reached the age of accountability. But God provided the remedy for our sins long before we entered the world and made it available to us. No one can justify himself on the ground of pre-existing sin and at the same time reject the plan of salvation as provided.

To do so contributes to the destruction of the very world that gives him sustenance and offends the very God who gives him all he has. The warning is plain: "Be not deceived; God is not mocked; for whatsoever a man soweth, that shall he also reap." (Gal. 6:7.)

The Principle of Completeness in Primal Creation

Having considered the need of law and of obedience right from the beginning, let us now take up the principle of completeness in primal creation. Before doing this, it is necessary to understand the attributes of God. We can only know them as revealed in His Word. Numerous passages show clearly that He is eternal (from everlasting to everlasting), omnipotent (almighty, not limited in authority or power), omnipresent (present everywhere at the same time), and

11

omniscient (knowing all things). He is infinite (no boundaries and no limits) and perfect in every way.

Previous to "the beginning", there was in existence <u>God and nothing</u>. He is about to create the finite world. What kind of world would He create? Would it be perfect and complete like the Creator, or an imperfect, incomplete world, having qualities of the sinful world in which we now live?

If we suppose that it was a world of incompleteness and imperfection, we are supposing that God created a condition which arose only <u>after sin entered the world</u>. The condition did not exist at the time of primal (first, original) creation (Gen. 1:1). Nothing in God's revealed Word can be construed to indicate that it did. Hence, if the world was imperfect and incomplete in the beginning, as some maintain, then this imperfection and incompleteness must have come from God, the Creator. If we establish such a supposition, we'll have to put it on the following basis: (1) God could produce in His works qualities which He does not possess Himself. (2) An unfinished work could come from God, who is Himself the perfection of completeness. (3) It is possible for God to change. (4) God could do all these things for His own glory.

Nothing in the Word established any of these propositions. We must conclude that they are all false. They could come only from a source of falsity. Not from God or from His Word, for the latter is like Himself. The perfect Creator could not at the beginning create an unfinished world, for incompleteness is not one of His attributes, nor is it consistent with His perfection. Only the human mind, perverted by sin, could come up with such an idea. We do not read anywhere in the Word that He ever worked by stages before sin entered the world.

You would have to base such an assertion from a subjective reading of God's Word rather than an objective reading. This means the reading of the Word for the purpose of adding something to it. A common example of this method is that of asserting that the first chapter of Genesis after the first verse is a description of the "method" or "process" of creation.

12

The Time Involved in Creation

How long did it take God to create the finite world, there being no sin?

There are two views of this, each of which is directly opposed to the other. One of them is the speculation that it required time of unknown and inconceivable length. This is the view that is almost universal today (but evolution is finally being exposed for its falsity). Sometimes the view is modified to the extent of admitting that God did not really require a long period of time, but this was in fact the method He actually used. It is usually presented as a philosophic or scientific concept of much importance. In this view, the emphasis is laid on its intellectuality. The view is in reality based upon an imperfect knowledge of the natural laws as applied to science. The natural laws as applied to science. It also overlooks the question of sin.

The Bible makes it clear in many passages that God required His children to do everything to His glory, even in such daily matters as eating and drinking (I Cor. 10:31). As God, He could not require His creatures to do everything to His glory unless He Himself was bound by the same law. (See Luke 10:16; John 13:20.) Hence, if God used time in creating the world, it was necessary for Him to do this to His glory. His word nowhere shows that He uses time to His glory, <u>except in dealing with the world after sin entered. He used time then to show His loving patience with those who sin against Him</u>. In this He glorifies Himself by showing long-continued love to His sinful creatures who do not love Him.

In the beginning, however, when He created the heavens and the earth, there was no sin. There was nothing in existence but God Himself. He had but one way apparent to us in which to glorify Himself, and that was through His work of creation. According to His Word, He created the world in a miraculous way instantaneously. Had He used time, it would have been wasted, because time was unnecessary. This would have been

13

dishonor to Himself, <u>and</u> <u>from</u> <u>Himself</u>! That would have been a far greater dishonor than for His sinful creatures to dishonor Him, thus dishonor from a sinful source. In the former case, God would have been dishonored <u>from</u> <u>a</u> <u>sinless</u> <u>source</u>, and that is wholly absurd.

The idea that God in creating the world previous to sin could use any length of time He chose is wholly false. It is the basis of theistic evolution, that false doctrine of the enemy, or Satan. If the world came into being through the natural process of evolution, it did not need a Creator. If it came from God, it came only by miraculous creation, which is the very antithesis of evolution. Theistic evolution, then, is a contradiction in terms. To maintain that evolution can be theistic is as inconsistent as to claim that a falsehood can be truth.

It is sometimes held that God created by stages through what is called "the process of creation." Anything in the nature of a process requires time. Processes are a very common thing in the natural world, which is the world of sin. It is the world we live in and experience. This, however, is a totally different world from the primal world before sin entered it. The Bible nowhere mentions or implies such a thing as processes in primal creation.

In preaching the gospel of salvation, we believe in the authority of the Scriptures (John 3:16; Romans 10:9, 10; and other passages) that anyone who in his heart believes on the Lord is immediately saved unto eternal life. Thus the sinner immediately becomes an immortal being, a new creature. The Lord Jesus, God the Son, was also the Creator of the physical world in the beginning (Col. 1:16). Shall we say He used aeons and aeons of time to create the world for man's abode and only an instant to create an immortal spirit?

The earth will wax old like a garment (Psalm 102:26; Hebrews 1:10-12) and will finally pass away (Matthew 5:18). An immortal life will endure forever. Shall it be said that it took aeons of time to create the world as a place where man could fall into sin and die, yet only an instant to create an immortal life? Did it take infinitely more time for God to create the inanimate world which will pass away than to create an immortal life enduring forever?

We must make a clear distinction between primal creation and the reconstruction of the world as a consequence of sin. The failure to do this has been a source of much confusion in understanding Genesis. Those who hold to the view that the first chapter of Genesis after the first verse is an account of the method of creation have failed to make this distinction. Such a view brings confusion into account and makes it impossible to understand creation. This makes it also impossible to harmonize Genesis with other passages on the basis of inspiration. More than this, it dishonors God by implying that He lacked either the power or the wisdom to create the world as He wanted it in the first place. It assumes that God did the work of the enemy. Such speculation is greatly in error, because it fails to consider the problem of sin. This subject of "creation by stages or processes" before sin entered the world will be taken up in later chapters.

Miraculous Finite Creation

Let us now take up the second view; namely, it was <u>not</u> a time-consuming process. Let us consider instantaneous creation first on the basis of established law in the natural world. This phase of the subject is weightier than is commonly supposed, and it is quite generally overlooked.

The mathematical law expressing the relation between the time required to do a piece of work and the power applied is this: <u>The Time Is Inversely Proportional to the Power</u>. In other words, the greater the power, the less the time required. For example, if it takes one man one day to do a piece of work, it will require 1/10 of a day for ten men to do it; it will require 1/100 of a day for 100 men; 1/1000 of a day for 1/000 men, and so on If the number of men is unlimited, the fraction of a day required by this same law will be 1 divided by infinity ($1/\infty$). The value of quantity, $1/\infty$, is zero. Thus, as the power increases when applied to a finite work, the time diminishes until finally with unlimited power the time is reduced to zero; that is, <u>no</u> <u>time</u> <u>at</u> <u>all</u>.

Therefore, could infinite power be applied in such a manner as to consume time? Theoretically, it might be applied in part to some other work, such as overcoming resistance or opposing some other force. Or a part of the power might remain idle. It should be noted, however, that these conditions all imply an imperfect world. If the power were working under perfect conditions, there could be none of the conditions of opposition nor of ineffective application of power in any way which would consume time. Hence, when unlimited or infinite power is applied to a finite work, no time is consumed. The work is done instantly. This is the law concerning the operation of unlimited or infinite power as applied to a finite work under natural law in a perfect world.

Let us return to the question, How long did it take God to create the finite world? The power applied was infinite. The conditions under which the power was applied were perfect in all respects. So, on the basis even of natural law, we know that <u>no</u> <u>time</u> <u>at</u> <u>all</u> <u>was</u> <u>consumed</u>.

Is there not the least possibility that God consumed time in the primal creation of Genesis 1:1? No, none whatsoever; because before primal creation there was nothing in existence in the form of a physical world involving time. God alone existed. There was no possibility of hindrance of any kind from without, because there was nothing without. If God had consumed time, He would have been working against Himself. That would make Him a God of confusion, and not the God of order that He is shown to be in the Bible.

Some assume and conclude that even in primal creation before sin entered the world God used time because of His infinite character. This is a form of philosophical reasoning based on the assumption that time exists in eternity. While sequence does imply time as an essential, it is not true that time has existence in eternity. Time is measurable and finite; eternity is immeasurable and infinite. It is, therefore, not only impossible to measure eternity but also impossible for the finite mind to think in terms of eternity. Sequence does not apply to eternity because time has no existence there. Time must be measured by motion, which involves matter; for matter is essential to the measurement of motion in the finite world. As matter had no existence prior to primal creation, there was no possibility of measuring time. The attempt to understand eternity by introducing finite terms is vain.

In the application of infinite power to a finite work, the time required must be equal to zero, which is no time at all. If time be assumed, it detracts from the power. As the assumed time increases, the power must diminish until with infinite time the power is reduced to zero. Therefore, if primal creation extended over aeons of time, it follows that the power involved was reduced to practically nothing. Such power could not possibly be that of the Creator, who has infinite power. It would be the power of a creator having human attributes. This is the god of the modernist, and it is also the basis of evolution, which is the basis of false religion.

Previous to the beginning, there was no time; it was eternity. God would have had to create time as His first act in order to be able to use it. Since He is omnipotent, He had the power to create the world instantaneously; any use of time would have been wasted time. It follows, then, that speculation about aeons would require that God create time in order to waste it.

The reason this speculation is erroneous is due largely to looking at primal creation from the wrong point of view. In viewing from the present back to the beginning, as is done, we necessarily pass through a world smitten by the cumulative effects of sin. Such imperfection obscures the view and results in confusion and darkness. Instead of this, we should choose a point of view before the beginning, and from this point of perfection in eternity look forward to the perfection of primal creation. Thus, by looking from perfection to perfection, it is possible for us to see clearly.

17

The conclusion, then, is that there was but one way in which God could have created the world in the beginning; that was by miraculous and instantaneous creation. It required no time because God had the power to do it instantly; there was no other way in which He could have worked to His glory according to His own revealed Word.

The God of the Bible is the God of miracles, not of evolution and processes. Miracles are unwelcome to the natural mind in the world under sin, because they deprive sinful man of his opportunity for self-glory. Miracles defy all human comprehension. They bring finite, sinful man face to face with his helplessness.

The question, Where did God come from? is sometimes asked ignorantly or even presumptuously. This question cannot be answered understandingly by finite man, because the answer pertains to the infinite. In the beginning God was already in existence. He is eternal; therefore, He had no beginning. He exists in eternity, but eternity has no beginning either, for eternity has no time. The full answer to the question transcends human comprehension. (See Fig. 2.1; 2.2; 2.3.)

MATHEMATICAL PRINCIPLES

Source: L. Allen Higley, <u>Science</u> and <u>Truth</u>, New York: Fleming H. Revell Co., 1940.

2.1

Mathematical law is always dependable, because it is a part of the created world; and it has not been marred since creation. We know this, because it is still in agreement with itself and with all related truth. It is in keeping with law and order as against disorder and confusion. The following are important applications of such law:

I. The principle of addition as involved in evolution:
    $1+1 = 2$ is always true   (1.)
    But, $1+1=2+$ is always false   (2.)
    For, reducing, $2=2+$ (3.)
    And, $0=+$ (4.)

Thus, a quantity of unknown value added to either side of a true equation without being accounted for gives an impossible result. Such a thing, applied generally, would bring confusion and disorder into the world. The world would be constantly in danger of having something arise out of nothing in lawless disorder. Such a world could not stand.

The principle involved here is identical with that assumed in evolution regarding the origin of life. Also with that regarding the speculation that the higher forms of life arose out of lower forms.

II. The principle of amount of time involved in primal, finite previous creation previous to sin:

Let X=any finite thing to be accomplished, as that of creating the world.

And, ∞=the infinite power of the Creator who brought it into being.

A. According to fixed law.

Then, $X/\infty = 0$, the time required $\qquad$ (5.)

Primal, finite creation, therefore, consumed no time.

2.2

B. According to the assumption involving time of definite length, t.

Then, $X/\infty = t$, the time required by the assumption. $\qquad$ (6.)

Substituting the value of X/∞ given in (5.), we obtain $0 = t$. $\qquad$ (7.)

The result is impossible. The principle is the same as in (4.)

C. According to speculations involving aeons, or practically infinite time (∞').

On this basis, $X/\infty = \infty'$ the time required. (8.)

Substituting the value of X/∞ as above in (5.), we obtain $0 = \infty'$. $\qquad$ (9.)

The result is the height of absurdity. The principle is the same as in (4.), and (7.)

The true equation showing the relation between power and work that consumes infinite time, instead of the false equation (8.), is $X/0 = \infty$. (10.)

That is, if finite work is to be done in infinite time, the power must be equal to zero. But, with no power, no work it possible.

Therefore, according to this speculation, there could be no creation at all.

20

Equation (8.), as applied to the assertion is theistic evolution, namely that in creating the world, God worked through aeons of time, simply means that such a god has no power at all. Such a being is to be wholly disregarded. It could not possibly be the God of the Bible. Theistic evolution is the height of absurdity.

It has no place in the world of reality.

III. The principle of time involved in eternal creation including man as a being eternally like God:

Let ∞" = any infinite thing to be accomplished, as that of creating the new heaven and the new earth, including man as eternally like God.

And ∞ = the infinite power of the Creator who will bring it into being.

Then $\infty"/\infty = t$, the time required. (11.)

Hence, for God to create the eternal world, including man as eternally like God, requires a period of time which is, of course, finite.

This was the obvious reason for the creation of the finite world involving time. It is a necessary part of eternal creation, even without the hindrance due to sin.

Summary:

I. It is impossible to add anything unknown to that which is true and still retain truth.

Hence, to add to the unknown values of the conjectures of evolution the objective truth of the natural world is to render the result a confusion.

II. In the creation of the finite world, with its perfection conditioned on the course of free-will creatures, time was not consumed. The introduction of time, whether literal days, or aeons, renders an impossible result.

21

The Bible does mention, however, 7 days. This time cannot refer to primal creation previous to sin. It refers to reconstruction after sin had marred the world.

Thus, Biblical truth and mathematical law are in agreement.

III

PRIMAL CREATION
(Genesis 1:1)

"In the beginning God created the heavens and the earth." (NASV.) This is the very first statement in the Bible. No such sublime words are to be found in any literature except the Bible itself. They are too profound for the deepest philosopher, too accurate for the most learned scientist. Yet, they are simple enough for a child to understand.

Only ten words in the English translation, yet they are more profoundly significant, perhaps, than any other statement in the entire Bible. Doubtless no other statement in the Bible is read so superficially or with so little concern as to its true meaning.

The uneducated regard it as too deep for them, so they think that they need not be concerned. The educated unbeliever regards it as largely mythical. It serves him mainly as a suggestion in his thinking about beginnings of any kind. It does not occur to him that the first statement of the Bible rightly understood would help him to obtain an intelligent understanding of a great number of other things of real concern to him.

The average educated believer, however, fails to understand even more perhaps than the others, if we take into consideration his light and his opportunity for understanding. As he reads those first words of the Bible, he seldom prays or meditates on them. He does not seek the meaning that lies beyond him; he is not aware that if he understood the meaning better, he would be a better servant of the God he worships and seeks to serve. Usually, when he reads these words and wonders what they may mean, he consoles himself by saying that it does not matter anyway, as long as he believes the Gospel. The Gospel is of interest because it touches his own life. The first verse of Genesis is less interesting because it is too remote from the

23

world in which he lives. If he does not give the matter any serious thought, he turns to secular science and philosophy to find enlightenment. He has been told that these are learned subjects, which, of course, will lend enlightenment. When, after a time, he finds that these fail to satisfy, he neglects the subject entirely. He is unaware that in doing this he is neglecting the very foundation of his faith and of all that he holds worth while in it.

"In the beginning God created the heavens and the earth." Let us consider these words, first of all, on the merits of the Bible itself. After this, applications may be made toward understanding subsequent Scriptures, and towards understanding secular subjects more fully, especially their foundation.

"In the beginning." Beginning of what? The beginning of time. Time is a measured portion of duration. This, then, was the beginning of the finite world, the world in which we live, even the very world in which it was possible for sin to enter. What was there before the beginning? Just God and nothing else. He exists in eternity. Hence, prior to the beginning there was eternity, but no time. Since time had a beginning, will it also come to an end? Yes, this is what the Bible reveals to us, though without this revelation we should not know. When time comes to an end, we shall enter upon eternity.

What are we to understand by the word "God"? This word has many meanings. What does it mean here? That God was in existence before the beginning is plainly implied in the statement under consideration. He is the only true God (Isaiah 45:22; 46:9). God is so far above us that we can have but little comprehension of Him (Isaiah 55:8,9). What are His attributes? How may we know them? Not by human ingenuity, but by direct revelation from Himself. Otherwise, we should not know at all. Human attempts to describe God always fail because the finite can never encompass the infinite. He has revealed Himself that we may serve Him better, not that we may satisfy our curious mind. According to His revelation, God is perfect in all respects. He is eternal, omnipresent, omnipotent, and

24

omniscient. He is a triune being consisting of Father, Son, and Holy Spirit. The Hebrew word for God used here is "Elohim." It is a plural noun with a singular verb. His attributes are plainly stated in the Bible. This is His Word, the only book we have in which His attributes are revealed to us. The revelation was made for our guidance.

God is all light.[2] There is no darkness at all in Him. We know that He could not have created darkness in the beginning, because He could not bring into being something at variance with His own attributes. Darkness is in direct opposition to His nature. If He created it, then His world would be in opposition, and it could not stand.

He is omnipresent.[3] Since God is everywhere present, there is no possibility of hiding from Him. No possibility of doing anything not seen by Him. Our every act, deed, and thought is known to Him. How foolish, then, to presume that we could think and plan anything in our own way unnoticed by Him. The willful sinner wants a God of limited light and limited presence, because he wants to find a place in which to hide from God.

Since He is omnipotent[4], there is no limit to His power in a world that is wholly obedient to Him. In primal creation there was nothing to oppose His holy will, hence no occasion for delaying the execution of His will. He worked miraculously and instantaneously. At that time there was no possibility of working through natural means, as in our time of sin. There was no sin in the beginning nor, indeed, any natural world. He accomplished His will without opposition, so the execution of His will is not called <u>work</u> in primal creation because there was nothing to overcome. He did not <u>rest</u> from His activity when it was done. Until sin and opposition to His will entered the world, there was no need for rest.

---

[2] I John 1:5; Isaiah 60:19.
[3] I Kings 8:27; Job 23:8,9; Psalm 139:7-10; Proverbs 15:3.
[4] Gen. 17:1, 28:3; Ex. 6:3; Job 9:4-13; Matt. 19:26.

God is omniscient[5]. He knows all things, even the end of everything from the beginning. Nothing is hidden from Him.

What light does all this throw on creation in the beginning (Gen.1:1)? Before the beginning, as already stated, there was the omnipresent, omnipotent, omniscient God, perfect and complete in all respects. Again let us ask, What kind of world must the world that He is about to create necessarily be? Perfect and complete or imperfect and incomplete?

Here is where speculation so often enters. When the speculator supposes incompleteness and imperfection, he is supposing a condition known to exist at the present time when sin is in the world. This could not have been the case in primal creation, because there was no sin then to cause imperfection or incompleteness of any kind. Even God could not produce what is in opposition to Himself. The Perfect One cannot create anything imperfect and still retain perfection. The Omnipotent One cannot create an incomplete work and still retain His omnipotence. It is a similar truth to state that the Holy God cannot create or commit sin and still retain holiness, that He could not disregard the necessity of paying the penalty of man's sin and still retain His justice.

There has been much philosophizing as to the "mode of creation" of the natural world in an attempt to show that if God chose, He could work through stages of imperfection and finally attain perfection. This speculation is wholly secular and evil in its effects. No attempt is made by those who speculate in this manner to show how God is glorified in it. No heed whatsoever is given to the divine command requiring us to glorify Him in all things. Thus it is in reality nothing short of sin to hold such a view. Knowingly or unknowingly, those who hold it bring God down in their thinking to a merely human plane.

Of necessity, we must conclude that all speculation regarding the origin and history of the world previous to the time

---

[5] I Sam. 16:7; I Kg. 8:39; II Chr. 16:9; Ps. 33:13, 44:21.

of man is entirely futile. Any such speculation is merely an attempt of an imperfect being to discover and reveal to the world what the Creator Himself has not seen fit to reveal beyond what is found in His Word. Who would be so presumptuous as to believe that this could be done? If it could be done, whom would it glorify, God or man? How could it be used to make man fear the righteousness and justice of God?

Next, consider how long God, the Infinite, takes to create the finite world from nothing. As has already been stated—when the power is increased, the time is proportionately diminished until, finally, with the application of infinite power it is reduced to zero, that is, <u>no</u> <u>time</u> <u>at</u> <u>all</u>. Time could not be consumed if applied to any <u>sum</u> of finite acts in a perfect world either. There would be no occasion for allowing a part of the power to stand idle, nor for any portion of the power to be consumed on opposing forces. In a perfect world there would be nothing to hinder in any way whatsoever. Infinite power would be applied to the finite act in a perfect manner, with the inescapable result that the act would be accomplished instantly.

Now let us consider further proof concerning this matter of God's creating the world out of nothing. The power was infinite and, therefore, unlimited. The work was finite, hence, limited. Since there was nothing in existence outside of God, there could be no possibility of resistance or opposition of any kind to cause a consumption of time. Nor could there be any possibility of having any portion of the power remaining idle; for this would be useless power, a thing that would detract from the perfection of the Creator. Such a thing would make God an inefficient being and would bring dishonor to His name.

He required man to do everything to His glory (I. Cor. 10:31). It is manifestly not credible that God would require man to comply with a rule which He Himself does not observe. Everything He does must bring honor to Himself, not dishonor.

In principle, it would be like His requiring man to abstain from sin while committing sin Himself. Such creation would be out of harmony with itself and for that reason would fall. This

27

would place the responsibility for failure with the Creator Himself.

God must of necessity, then, have created the world in the manner which would bring the most glory to Himself. Therefore, we know He did it miraculously and instantaneously. There was no other way for it to be done under the conditions then prevailing.

There is the idea advanced by many speculators that God as an infinite being has the power to use any method He chooses, even to that of consuming aeons of time. This idea is of purely human origin. It assumes a creator other than the God of the Bible. In the speculation no attempt is made to show how God is glorified. That is very conveniently avoided, for reasons which are obvious. Such speculation glorifies man, and does so at the expense of God's glory and power. Yes, this speculation would presume that the omnipotent Creator uses time needlessly in order to gratify the speculator's vanity.

In the creation, in the beginning, there was no sin. There was no method of creation by which God could be glorified except a miraculous, instantaneous one. A world thus created would also glorify its Creator at once, not lie useless for aeons. (Psalm 24:1 "world" tebel – habitable.)

What are we to understand by the word "created"? Here, again, we obtain most of our light from the Bible. We are now dealing with the word in its primal sense. This means bringing instantly into being something out of nothing. Such a thing can be done only by the one true Creator because He is the only being who is all-powerful and all-wise. For Him to make a finite thing out of nothing is a miracle and does not require time. Since the world was created out of nothing by the omnipotent Creator, it is easy to understand how the world came to be supplied with such vast energy, because it came from one who is Himself eternal power.

"The heavens and the earth." What is to be understood by words heavens and earth? Heavens refers to the physical universe, with all its unmeasured space and its uncounted millions of physical bodies. But since the physical world was created for the purpose of serving life, created life is a necessary part for its completion. This is perfection in the primal sense. It is the perfection alone which honors God (Isa. 45:18: "not in vain" (tohu – waste, empty).

It is not possible to understand how God could be glorified by first creating an imperfect and unfinished heaven, and then through stages of subsequent work during aeons and aeons of time finally bringing it to perfection; or or how could God be honored by allowing it to stand idle for further aeons before putting it to its intended use—the support of life. The idea that such a method of creation could have been used is not to be found anywhere in the Bible. It is a purely human concept. Its origin is secular. The purpose is to afford scope for vain speculation. God could no more use time needlessly and still retain His omnipotence than He could disregard the penalty of sin and still retain His justice.

What are we to understand by the word "earth" as used here? Clearly, we are to understand a complete and perfect earth just as we are to understand the physical heaven. Earth, as directly from the hand of the perfect Creator, would not be the earth if it were in a state requiring further work through untold aeons of time to bring it to a state of fitness for supporting life. This would be absurd and self-contradictory "process creation." This also is a human concept and one of pagan origin. It is not found anywhere in the Bible.

The earth was complete and perfect when created. It was filled with life, though, of course, not human life. Man, as it is revealed to us, was created long afterwards (Gen. 1:26-28). The earth contained plant and animal life. Also angelic life endowed with moral responsibility. We are told that when the earth was created, the angelic hosts sang (Job 38:4-7). Also that Lucifer (Isa. 14:12), before his fall, was in "Eden the garden of God." (Eze. 28:13,15.) Of course a garden contains plants, as the word signifies. Furthermore, we are told that this same garden of God contained trees (Eze. 31:8,9,16,18). This "Eden the garden of

God" was not the "garden eastward in Eden" (Gen. 2:8,15), where man was placed at the time of his creation. When Satan entered the latter, he had already fallen. The distinction between the two Edens is the distinction between primal creation, previous to the entrance of sin into the world, and the reconstructed world. This will be taken up later. Here, it is sufficient to observe that they were separated by a period of time of unrevealed length.

The evidence that plants existed previous to those mentioned on the third day is clearly implied in the latter (reconstructed world) account, Gen. 1:3f. The same thing is true of the animals mentioned on the fifth and sixth days. It is clear enough that the purpose of plants is to support other life. Hence, the two go together in creation. They also go with the meaning of the word earth. In the Genesis account of the Deluge (Noah's flood), the mention of destroying the earth because it was corrupt and full of violence means, of course, the earth with its life (Gen. 6:11,12). Likewise with many other passages. In the original Hebrew of Genisis 1:1 the same word is used for earth as occurs in Genesis 6:11,12 (Deluge). This implies an earth with living things in it right from the beginning. It certainly does not mean a hypothetical earth not yet in a condition to support life. In fact the Bible does not mention such an earth anywhere from Genesis to Revelation. The concept of a hypothetical earth not yet containing life is of evolutionary origin. It is wholly speculative.

Clearly, then, the earth mentioned in the first verse of Genesis was complete and perfect, filled with life. Since it had angelic life, it appears that the earth was created as an abode for angels. It contained the throne of Lucifer before his fall (Isa. 14:13).

The angels were present when the earth was created; hence they were created before the earth. We infer that the earth was created to be the throne of Lucifer. This seems to be very clearly implied in the statement of Lucifer: "I will exalt my throne above the stars of God: I will sit also upon the mount of the congregation, in the <u>sides of the north</u>[6]: I will ascend above the heights of the clouds; I will be like the most High." (Isa. 14:13,14; Exo. 13:21.) It was this unholy ambition that led to his fall.

From this we may conclude that the earth was created later than the heavens. This is confirmed by the fact that in the creation account the earth is mentioned <u>after</u> the heavens.

Let us now consider what is expressed and implied in the first verse of the Bible. Let us see, if possible, how far-reaching it is. It contains the concept <u>time</u>, as found in the phrase, "in the beginning." The concept <u>space</u> is found in the words "heaven and earth." It contains the concept <u>energy</u> as found in the words "God created." Time, space, and energy are the three basic units on which all science is built. Some scientists formerly added two more units, <u>matter</u> <u>and</u> <u>motion</u>, as coordinate with time, space, and energy. These two are really included in the first three units. Functioning heavenly bodies certainly include <u>motion</u>; also that the earth and the other heavenly bodies include <u>matter</u>. These basic units of science are accounted for here in the Bible and nowhere else. Man may discover existing truth, but he can never originate it. All true science must acknowledge this fact.

The origin of the heavenly bodies is found here. Also all of the laws governing their motion and their properties. The heat, light, and other forms of energy which they contain is also accounted for here. This is the very foundation of astronomy. All attempts to speculate on the origin of the heavenly bodies result in confusion. All human attempts to account for their energy and the laws governing them are wholly futile. The Bible alone gives us the basis for an adequate understanding.

---

[6] Psalm 48:2—"Beautiful in elevation, the joy of the whole earth, is Mount Zion, on the <u>sides of the north</u> (same Hebrew words)...."

The origin of the earth is here stated plainly. It was created. Hence, it could not have evolved into being from a nebulous cloud, nor through any other time-consuming process. None of the various hypotheses that attempt to account for the origin of the earth is of any value. All assume original matter, its vast energy, the laws which govern it, the design involved, and the power; yet they are without the least explanation or even intimation as to origins or causes of the functions. Furthermore, they all assume intelligence in the world long before any life of any kind could have appeared, according to the hypotheses.

All of the earth sciences rest upon the first verse of the Bible as their foundation. Here only is to be found an understanding of the intricacies which are involved. Here only is to be found the adequate cause of the effects which we study as science.

The origin of matter and of energy, together with the laws governing the latter, is to be found also in the beginning of the Bible. Here alone is to be found the ultimate origin of everything which is treated in physics and chemistry. All of the remarkable discoveries made in these sciences during the last two hundred years involved the problem of origins and hence lead directly to the Creator of all things. Only in the Bible do we find the solution and that in the very first verse. Physics and chemistry are helpless to account for origins, and so this phase of these subjects is almost wholly neglected in the presentation of the subject matter of these sciences.

Even life, by inference, is first mentioned in this very same verse. Therefore, we find that the beginning of biology is found here. No serious attempt is ever made in the modern study of biology to explain the origin of life on a scientific basis. The so-called explanations are mere idle speculations. Obviously, biology is helpless to explain the origin of life, because life cannot be defined. So far as biological definition is concerned, life is wholly a miracle. The question of origins is as much an enigma in biology as it is in the physical sense. In both cases the solution must be sought outside of the sciences as such.

It is universally true that all natural life must come from previous life of some kind. Obviously, the first natural life could not have come from previous natural life; nor could it have come from nothing. As it had to come from life of some kind, it must have come from supernatural life. Otherwise it would not have been in keeping with the law of cause and effect. Of necessity it had to come from the Creator Himself.

Thus, all natural sciences must depend upon the first verse of the Bible for an explanation of the existence of the things they have under investigation. It is true that many of these things are no longer in the perfect condition in which they first existed. The explanation for this change also is found in the Bible. This subject will be taken up in the following Chapter.

All this being true, why is it that the scientist of today is so often atheistic? This is because of the superficiality of his studies. He is too easily satisfied with surface appearances. In matters of ultimate cause and true origin he is too easily satisfied with speculations that do not explain. He needs the help that only the Bible can give. As long as he leaves God's name out of consideration in his treatment of science, he must be superficial.

It has only been during the past hundred years or so that scientists have so greatly ignored the Bible. Previous to this, most scientists were believers, and they took the Bible as their guide. Most prominent among these was Sir Isaac Newton, the greatest scientist of modern times, if not indeed of all times. He had a profound understanding of the Bible and lived accordingly. In fact, he wrote some valuable works on the Bible which are still read with profit. In our day, many scientists pay no attention to the Bible except to scoff at it. This accounts for their superficiality, also for some of their blunders.

"In the beginning God created the heavens and the earth." What simple words. Yet, how fraught with meaning. Here is found the first and greatest recorded miracle. It is the foundation not only of all science but of the Bible as well. The entire superstructure of the Bible rests upon this statement. If it could be proved that this is false, the remainder of the Bible would be open to question. All else that is recorded as miraculous would be open to explanation through evolution or other natural cause.

If it could be shown that the God of the first verse of the Bible is not the same as the God of the remainder of the Bible, then there would be in reality no triune God. There would be no Son and no Holy Spirit. Or it if could be shown that He changed His attributes after the first act of creation as recorded here, then there would be no real God at all. There would be no Creator to be feared because of His justice and power, nor to be loved because He first loved us.

Is it not easy to understand why the enemies of God have worked so hard to destroy this first verse of the Bible by perverting its meaning? Every subtlety has been resorted to in order to deceive, sometimes by misrepresentation, sometimes by substituting false light—misnamed science. Many, accepting this false light, have come to regard science as vastly superior to the Bible. It is quite possible to dwell upon speculation so constantly that one loses his power to evaluate it correctly. Then, in time, the speculation is held as fact. Many do this without realizing it. The tendency for one to follow this course is all the greater when nearly everybody else does it.

In this way, the eternal truth of God has been exchanged for the mere idle speculation of men who do not even agree among themselves. They are "ever learning, and never able to come to the knowledge of the truth" (II Tim. 3:7). This spirit has come to dominate the educated world so completely that one wonders where it will end. When most of the educated classes are so engrossed in false views as to have little concern for the truth, we should have grave concern for our future welfare.

The words in the first verse are even significant for what is not expressed. It does not begin with the expression "Let it be done," nor does it close with the observation "And God saw that it was good." These two expressions are used in most of the recorded acts of God found in the first chapter of Genesis.

God, who has a reason for everything He does, must have a reason for this. Let us see if we can find it. The expression "Let it be done" implies that the act involves overcoming a difficulty or obstacle of some kind. This is especially implied in the word let. For example, one may say, "Let me go," or "Let me come in." This is plainly a command to some one else involved in that which we wish to accomplish.

In primal creation with God and nothing, there was no other being external to Himself who could be addressed. Nor could there possibly have been any obstacle to overcome. There was no obstacle to what God wanted to do; He alone existed. Therefore the expression is not used. The evidence for primal creation is found in this very fact. The absence of any command is essential to the accuracy of the statement.

When primal creation was accomplished, God did not pronounce it good. Yet His acts were pronounced good no less than seven times in connection with His work during the course of the six days. Here, again, there must be a reason for the omission from the first verse. Let us inquire into the meaning of the word good. It is the antitheses of bad. If we speak, for example, of a good man or of a good child, we imply at the same time a contrast with other men or with other children who are not good. We also imply just as clearly that the man is not a perfect man nor the child a perfect child. They are neither at the top nor at the bottom of the scale. In a perfect world, however, all men and all children would be perfect and therefore equal. There would be no contrast and hence no occasion to call any one good. Nor indeed to call any one perfect, for this would be understood without expressing it in words.

So in primal creation, it was not possible to speak as good in comparison with some other world that was imperfect for any reason. Nor was it possible to call it good in comparison with some other world above it that was also perfect. The world mentioned was itself the only one. It is not called perfect, because this is to be understood. It came directly from the hand of the perfect Creator, and for this reason could have no imperfections of any kind. To speak of it as imperfect or incomplete in any way would be dishonoring God.

35

It is clear, then, why the first verse does not begin with the expression "Let it be done," nor end with the observation "And God saw that it was good." These expressions do not belong to primal creation in which everything was perfect. The verse gives evidence, then, of its inspiration both in what it states and in what it omits.

The verse is simple as well as profound and at the same time wholly true. It is simple enough for a child to understand, yet profound enough to baffle the most learned. Let us all profit from its great truth.

Even though the world was perfect in primal creation, it was nevertheless not to be everlasting. This is an important thing to observe. It was destined to fall under the influence of sin, which would bring it to a termination. That is why the first verse does not state that the heavens and earth would be eternal. Such a statement is not to be found in any other place in the entire Bible. God, in His omniscience, knew the end from the beginning. He knew the world He created would come to destruction through sin. The evidence of its partial destruction is found in the very next verse of Genesis and is further implied in many other references as will be shown in the next Chapter.

We are not left, however, without hope. God has revealed to us that finally when all sin is done away with, He will create a new heaven and a new earth that will stand forever.[7] Much of our suffering is our own fault. Although the trials under sin seem hard, a remedy has been provided.[8] Why do we not avail ourselves of the promises provided for us? We who are saved must not allow our eyes to become blinded by temporary suffering. Ahead will be an eternity of perfect joy. (See next page.)

---

[7] I Cor. 15:28; II Pet. 3:13; Rev. 21:1.
[8] John 3:16; and other passages.

FINITE and INFINITE CREATION
ETERNITY

I.	**PRIMAL FINITE CREATION** The Finite World Created (Gen. 1:1). Conditional Perfection (Isa. 14:12-14; Ezk. 28:13-15).

		Perfection Lost by Sin of Fallen Angels. (Isa. 14:13-15; Ezk. 28:15-17).		
		The Great Cataclysmic Judgment (Gen. 1:2). Water and Darkness Over Whole Face of the Earth		
The Reconstructed World	Conditional Perfection (Gen. 3:17).	(~4,000 B.C.) First Day. (Gen. 1:3-5) Light Called Good. Divided from Darkness. Day. Night.	Conditional Perfection (Gen. 3:17).	The Reconstructed World.
		Second Day. (Gen. 1:6-8) The Firmament Made.		
		Third Day. (Gen 1:9-13) Seas. Dry Land. Plants. All Made.		
		Fourth Day. (Gen. 1:14-19) Lights Made. Sun. Moon. Stars. Signs. Seasons. Days. Years.		
		Fifth Day. (Gen. 1:20-23) Animals Created and Blessed		
		Sixth Day. (Gen. 1:26-31) Man Created and Blessed. All God Made Called Very Good.		
		Seventh Day Blessed and Sanctified.		
	Under Sin	Fall of Man (Gen 3:6). Perfection Lost (Gen. 3:7-19).	Under Sin	
		The Flood. Judgment for Sin (Gen. 6 and 7).		
		Sixth Thousand Years Drawing to an End. Lord's Return (Mt. 24:30; and II Pet. 3:8-10).		
		The Tribulation (Mt. 24:21)		
		Seventh Thousand Years: Millennium (Rev. 20:4)		
		Great White Throne Judgment. (Rev. 20:11-15)		

II. ETERNAL, INFINITE CREATION.
A New Heaven and A New Earth Finally Created (Isa. 65:17).
Time and the Finite World Have Passed Away.
(Rev.21:1; Isa. 65:17).
Eternal Perfection a Reality (Isa. 65:18, 19).

Eternity
God and His Eternal, Perfect World

Fig. 3.1. FINITE and INFINITE CREATION

Source: L. Allen Higley, <u>Science</u> <u>and</u> <u>Truth</u>, New York: Fleming H. Revell Co, 1940.

IV

THE GREAT CATACLYSMIC JUDGMENT
(Genesis 1:2)

Could the world ever have gone through a period of greater destruction than that in Noah's time? This is a most important question. A clear understanding of it is essential to a true comprehension of the Bible and of science also. An understanding of it involves the problem of sin, a subject which the Bible constantly emphasizes, although science persistently evades it.

Since the middle of the nineteenth century, most scientists have quite generally assumed that no destruction of magnitude, not even the Deluge, ever took place at any time. They profess to disbelieve in destructions of cataclysmic proportions. During this time the more sincere Bible students have accepted the Deluge as a fact; but they have regarded this as the only great disaster to the earth as a whole. Even some of these assert that the Deluge was limited to the region of western Asia.

Diligent inquiry into the subject demands emphasis upon the facts rather than the theories. Facts as referred to here include the truths revealed in the Bible and also verified by knowledge gained through science. The Bible, which is our chief reference, must be taken to mean what it states and nothing else. It must be read in its most obvious meaning based on the context and not in the light of popular speculation.

About a century ago it was generally held in science that the world had passed through many cataclysms. Some even held that the destruction was of such magnitude that all life was destroyed repeatedly and that it had to be recreated after each destruction.

All were agreed that the evidence of destroyed life was clearly found in the fossils. This evidence has become more

39

convincing than ever in the light of subsequent discoveries. In the light of this, it is only natural to ask, Why is this view not more generally accepted?

The answer to this is found in evolution, a certain form of fanciful speculation misnamed science. Evolution is purely speculation. It is pseudo-science, because it is directly opposed to the clearly observed facts and definitely established laws of science as well as directly opposed to the clear statements of the Bible. Those upholding evolution speculate boldly concerning the origin and propagation of life and then call this speculation science. Yet this is not the field of science but of religion. Since evolution runs counter to the bible in its every aspect, it is really nothing but fanciful speculation in the field of false religion. To many of its adherents it is religion itself and must be upheld with fanatical zeal.

Less than two hundred years ago certain men in science developed evolutionary speculation in connection with investigation in geology. They either took no interest at all in the Bible or arbitrarily opposed it because of unbelief. In order to make their speculation look plausible, they presumptuously asserted that the extensive fossil record did not really represent destruction at all, but instead, the ordinary course of life such as it is at present, spread over a long period of time. Charles Lyell was outstanding in this speculation and is regarded as its originator, although he was not the first to suggest it.

Every effort has been made to place this speculation on a scientific basis. Yet it has failed completely. Instead of acknowledging the failure and searching further for the truth, science so-called has accepted it without proof. As a result, in nearly everything written on the subject, evolution is taken as a fact, no proof evidently being thought necessary. Thus those not familiar with the subject are greatly mislead.

It is not difficult to understand why this false speculation has spread so universally during the past 150 years. The church has declined during this period; it has ceased to set forth the true doctrine of sin and its consequences. Out of this has grown a false religion seeking to set forth mostly pleasure with few if any consequences for disobedience to divine law. As a result, in the twentieth century the church has quite generally professed little belief in punishment for sin, past, present, or future. Of course, it has ceased to have any regard for a flood of any kind as a judgment affecting the entire world. Naturally, it welcomes anything that supports this view and accepts it without proof. Thus, strange though it may seem, the church has been the strongest factor in spreading the evolutionary phase of false science.

Evolution and cataclysms are mutually opposed. If one is true, the other must be false. Cataclysms are based directly on sin, the very thing that evolution evades or seeks to set aside by denying its existence.

As evolution has spread, cataclysms have been set aside without consideration. Merely setting aside the idea of cataclysms, however, has not in any sense altered the facts on which cataclysms are based. These facts can be explained only on the basis of world-wide destruction. All attempts to explain them on any other basis has been at the expense of intellectual integrity. The result has been very unsatisfactory.

When the evolutionary theory was put forth, the world's ablest scientists were fully convinced that the fossils found widely distributed in the rock formation constituted the plainest objective proof of correspondingly widespread disaster. As fossils were found in various horizons and in various kinds of sedimentary rock formed under different conditions, they naturally concluded that there had been a series of disasters. They set forth the idea that each disaster had resulted in the total destruction of life from the earth. Of course, this could not be proved. They had been taught to accept the Bible, and they believed in special creation. So they concluded that God re-created life after each of the total destructions.

This view was not convincing because it was not confirmed by the Bible. Nor could it be fully established through science. As leadership in science changed in the years following, belief in evolution arose in the place of belief in cataclysms. Thus, the fact of creation, which is Biblical, was first modified by misinterpretation which was thought to be Biblical; and then this was replaced by the fiction of evolution. The fossil evidence in the rocks shows extensive destruction of life brought about suddenly and violently. The evidence is fully convincing. Evolution has no explanation to offer other than groundless speculation. Such weighty evidence against evolution is evaded because evolution is helpless to meet it.

It is not within the limits of this presentation to set forth the fossil and the physical evidence of cataclysmic destruction which is so unmistakably shown in the rocks. The facts found are so clear and also so unusual that even evolutionists have reported them many times as a part of field discovery. They have seldom tried to explain them and even then only through speculation. The chief one of these speculations is that of uniformitarianism advanced by Lyell, as already referred to.

The fact of the extensive destruction of life is clear. It is beyond dispute. The next essential thing to determine is whether or not all of it could have taken place at the time of the Flood. There are very few who assert that the destruction all took place at this time. The view that it did is highly theoretical and unconvincing from both the Scriptural and the scientific standpoint.

The view overlooks the fact that the Bible records another flood at an earlier time. This flood is mentioned in verse 2 of the first chapter of Genesis and is also clearly implied in verses 6, 7, and 9. Although the word flood does not appear in verse 2, the context clearly implies that all plant and animal life was destroyed. The reason this flood is overlooked is that this chapter is often mistakenly regarded as a detailed account of what is thought to be the process of creation. The justification of the term <u>flood</u> is amply found in the account of the reconstruction which followed it.

Only a brief consideration of the errors of process creation need be presented in this connection. Creation, in its primal sense, means bringing into being something out of nothing. In its very nature this must be a miracle. This fact excludes all possibility of creation being a process. Furthermore, the fact that the God of the Bible is a God of order and not of confusion precludes the speculation that what verse 2 referred to is a description of the earth in an early stage of creation. The speculation that God first created an imperfect world as the beginning stage of a <u>process</u> of <u>creation</u> is equivalent to asserting that God lacked both the wisdom and the power to create the world as He wanted it in the first place. The speculation that the perfect Creator brought into being an imperfect world is wholly absurd. It dishonors God and makes Him a different being from the Creator of the Bible. It also violates definitely established law as shown in Chapter II (Miraculous Finite Creation). Process creation, therefore, is a distinct contradiction in terms. It makes the God of the Bible a god of theistic evolution and also the creator of sin, as will be shown.

No creative act of God could possibly have produced the conditions described in verse 2. These conditions were a result of great cataclysmic destruction, a judgment due to sin of the most grievous kind. The conditions mentioned account for the great destruction of life shown in the fossils and also for the devastation extended over a period of time. It is very clear from the objective evidence found in the rock formations. It is also confirmed by the Scriptures. This period as a whole is represented in a way by the time-table of geology; but it cannot be divided into distinct ages. The division of the geological time-table into ages is based entirely on evolution. Since the speculation on which evolution rests if false, the theory of ages must also be false.

In the present century there have been only a few individuals who have held that the earth has been subjected to catastrophic destruction on a world-wide scale. Among this number only a very few advanced the claim that all of the destruction took place at the time of Noah's Flood. The assertion that it did is advanced on theoretical grounds. None of the advocates of this theory has ever met the many objections to it. Some of these objections are the following:

(1) If nearly all of the fossils were formed at the time of this Flood, why was not man fossilized also? At that time there were unquestionably many millions of people, certainly a sufficient number for very extensive fossilization. The human body is quite as susceptible to fossilization as is that of the animal. If this particular Flood theory were true, both man and animals should be found fossilized together in large numbers. Instead of this, it is the animals that are found fossilized extensively but man scarcely at all. Evidence that the animals were fossilized extensively at a time earlier than the time of a man is seen in the fact that animal fossils are found in large numbers only at horizons below that of man, and greater depth is proof of greater age. This is further confirmed by the fact that at the top horizon where man is found fossilized to some small extent the animals are likewise only slightly fossilized. The reason for this agreement is clear. Both man and animal were fossilized in this meager way since the Flood. As this has been a time of unfavorable conditions for fossilization, few fossils of any kind are found and all forms of life have been affected somewhat alike.

(2) According to the Flood theory, how are we to account for the great variety of conditions under which the fossils were formed? For example, there are found in some places as many as a hundred beds of coal all superposed (layered) and yet interbedded in some regions with shale, sandstone, limestone, and salt, all highly stratified (alternate layers) because all of these formations were deposited by water. Some of these beds of coal contain, at the bottom, trees carbonized in their natural state; and these same beds as well as many others contain fossil ferns in which the fronds lie spread out in a natural position, thus proving that the plants were fossilized right where they grew and were not drifted into a heap by wave action. This proves that there were successive periods of time long enough at least for the growth of the successive generations of plants out of which the

coal was formed. Assuming that plants grew then as they do now under similar conditions, the time necessary for the growth of the plants alone was many thousands of years. To this must be added the time necessary for the formation of the rock and the salt between the beds of coal, which was probably still longer, since limestone is a very slow-forming rock. The period of transition from the deposition of one kind of rock to that of the next in the succession may also have been very long.

Coal is definite evidence of a mild climate, essential for the growth of the plants forming the coal. The interbedded layers of salt are equally definite evidence of a hot, arid climate, necessary for the evaporation of saline water from which the extensive beds of salt were deposited. The salt deposit of great thickness is itself evidence of thousands of years of time; for this was required to evaporate the water from which the salt was deposited. The transition from one kind of climate to its opposite and then back again is further evidence of a long period of time. Deposits of gypsum are sometimes found between the interbedded layers of coal and salt. The gypsum deposit bears unmistakable evidence of deposition from water, as does the salt. A simple calculation based on the solubility of these two compounds shows the volume of water necessary to hold in solution the salt and gypsum found in the deposit. The time necessary to evaporate this water must have been many thousands of years or more.

The total time involved in the formation of coal, gypsum, and salt layers just set forth is enormously greater than that of the period of the Flood.

(3) The Flood theory would lead to the absurdity of demanding opposite climates in the same place at practically the same time.

(4) Both gypsum and salt beds require inland seas detached from the ocean and an arid climate over a long period of time to effect their deposition. These conditions are wholly inconsistent with the conditions necessarily prevailing during a period of flood.

(5) No coal beds have ever been known to contain human fossils of any kind. Many of these fossils, such as artifacts and those made of gold, are as imperishable as anything, especially when covered up and protected from the action of the atmosphere. Such fossils as these would have survived the Flood and would be found as securely covered and preserved as the coal. The two should be found together, because the conditions for forming the one would form the other also. The fact that they are not found together is proof that they did not exist together. As coal is always found below human fossils, we can know that the coal was formed at a much earlier time.

(6) The time covered by the Flood was altogether too short to account for the outstanding facts of physical destruction found in the rock formations, to say nothing of the very extensive destruction of plant life and the preservation of it in the form of coal.

(7) Evidence of antediluvian man has been found on or near the present surface of the earth. This shows that the Flood did not destroy everything and bury it at all depths in the form of fossils. A Flood of such destruction as would account for practically all fossils that have been found would have destroyed every evidence of pre-Deluge civilization too.

There are reasons for concluding that some of the Egyptian pyramids now standing, and also some structures in Yucatan, were built before the Flood, if the Ussher[9] dates are accepted. These dates have been established by men of the ablest scholarship, though this fact is very commonly overlooked. They have been confirmed as <u>approximately</u> correct by scientific calculations based on astronomical phenomena.

---

[9] James Ussher (1581-1656), Irish dignitary of the church of England and Biblical scholar, who established a long-accepted chronology for the Old Testament.

46

(8) If the Flood theory were true, we should find every form of life fossilized in every horizon in which sedimentary rocks are found. This is definitely not the case.

(9) In certain regions in California there are trees living today known to be more than three thousand years old. Some of these trees are asserted to be more than four thousand years old. The Flood took place over 4,300 years ago. These plants, therefore, have been living during nearly the entire period since the Flood. They are rooted in soil older than they are. This soil lies over rock still older than the soil; for the soil was formed from the rock. The rock contains fossils formed under a variety of conditions requiring considerable time. To this time, add that required for forming the rock out of the sediment composing it; also the time required for the rock to disintegrate into the soil in which the tree as seedlings grew.

The question is, How long a time elapsed between the destruction of the fossilized forms of life found in the rocks, and the living forms now growing above these fossils? To claim that the time from the Flood to the seedlings was long enough to account for the formation of the fossils, the rock, and the soil is in no sense convincing; for the time for the former was only several hundred years at most.

In light of these facts, it is certain that the great period of fossilization was not at the time of the Deluge. Nor could it have been during the period between the creation of man and the Deluge; for just as in the period from the Deluge to the present, the time was much too short and the conditions for fossilization were not favorable.

The time from the creation of man to the Deluge was especially a time of tranquillity. It was not a time of destruction such as is necessary for fossilization. Hence, even if there were no other way of knowing when the period of great fossilization was, we should know by elimination that it was before the time of man. It may be shown on geological evidence alone that the six days were not "Geological Ages." On linguistic and other grounds they are shown to be literal days. Hence, the period of extensive fossilization was previous to the six days of Genesis.

At this point a difficulty may arise with some who are very conscientious. The one who has always believed that the plants and animals mentioned in the six days were the first in existence may hesitate to accept any findings of science to the contrary. If we accept from science decisive light on the Scriptural account of creation, it implies that the Scriptural account is incomplete and must be supplemented by modern science in order to be understood. It implies also that the Scriptural account of creation was not correctly understood until recent times, and that it is unsatisfactory of itself for twentieth century enlightenment. The consecrated Christian hesitates also in accepting from science light that is of vital importance on a Scriptural subject. He hesitates because it comes from unbelievers, or from those who, even at best, are indifferent to the Scriptures as authority. It may justly be feared that the evidence presented may be incomplete, or that it may need revision after further discoveries are made. For, after all, science is only a human conception of what is regarded as true.

Our sympathy should go out to those of this position. It is always dangerous to settle, on purely scientific ground, matters of vital importance in the Scriptures. This tends to make the Bible humanistic. It tends to subordinate the Bible to science, to subordinate the eternal truth to the temporal truth. We have no sympathy whatsoever with such exaltation of science at the expense of the Inspired Word.

Therefore, let us turn to the Bible itself for the evidence that plants and animals were in existence previous to those mentioned specifically in the account of the six days.

"In the beginning God created the heavens and the earth." Clearly, the omnipotent and perfect Creator could, and of necessity would, create only a perfect world. Anything short of this would not be a miracle, but a process. It would mean that infinite power stopped short of its purpose without a reason. No true servant of God would knowingly rob the Creator of His glory by regarding creation a mere process instead of a miracle.

A perfect world must be a complete world. Since the purpose of the world was the support of life, the world would not be complete until it had life on it. What need would there be for creating an empty world and then to stand lifeless and, therefore, useless for ages and ages?

"And the earth was (became) waste and void; and darkness was upon the face of the deep." The translation, "the earth became waste and void," is preferable to "the earth was without form and void." The verb used here in the Hebrew is hayethah. It can be translated either way. "Became" is more fully in keeping with the context and with other related passages of Scripture.[10] Isaiah 45:18 states that God created the earth not a waste, and that He formed it to be inhabited. Since the earth was created not a waste, and it is declared to have been in that condition afterward (v.2), it follows that it became a waste.[11]

"Waste" and "void" are translated from the original "tohu wabohu." Both times this word combination is used, it describes a condition of judgment (Gen. 1:2; Jer. 4:23). Any other interpretation of the phrase violates the most obvious usage of language. The interpretation that it is a description of an unfinished world in process of creation is illogical, absurd, and unscriptural. If it meant unfinished, it would have to say so in order to be accurate. Inspiration demands this. For example, who would even think of speaking of a building or anything else under construction and therefore unfinished as waste and void, or

---

[10] The word hayethan in Genesis 1:2 and Genesis 3:20 comes from the Hebrew verb "hayah" and is translated "became" in A Hebrew and English Lexicon by Brown, Driver, and Briggs. Other forms of the Hebrew verb "hayah" are found in Genesis 2:7, 10; Genesis 4:2; Exodus 4:3; and I Samuel 22:2 and are translated "became" by Brown, Driver, and Briggs.

[11] "Hebrew has no "tenses" . . . a verb is indicated by its context." The Essentials of Biblical Hebrew by Kyle M. Yates.

as <u>without</u> <u>form</u> <u>and</u> <u>void</u>? It is well established custom, however, to speak of the ruin and destruction caused by a tornado or a hurricane as waste and void, because it plainly means that life and material things once in a useful state have been destroyed.

The expression, "God created the earth not a waste," is a clear implication that it was created with life. And the expression of Isaiah 45:18, "He formed (not created) it to be inhabited," implies further that the life created in the beginning was destroyed. That which in the beginning (Gen. 1:1) was created perfect with life was later (during reconstruction week) "formed" for the purpose of being inhabited.

After the plants of the third day were called into being, it was called good. Since good is the antithesis of evil, it is clear that calling these plants into being was pronounced good only by reason of contrast with the preexisting plants that had fallen under the influence of sin.

After the animals were created on the fifth day, God called it good just as He had done on the third day with the plants. This implies that there had been other animals before these that had fallen under sin and that this was evil. There is a close analogy in this respect between the animals and the plants. In the case of the plants on the third day, God commanded the <u>earth</u> to bring them forth <u>after</u> <u>their</u> <u>kind</u>. The command was not addressed to the plants, but to the earth instead. It was the earth that was to bring them forth in this manner. Of course the seeds and roots left from the great cataclysm were already in the ground or earth. Since God is perfect in all respects, His creation is the same. Plants must, of necessity, reproduce their own kind; otherwise the Creator would be a being of confusion instead of order and His world could not stand. When the first man and woman were commanded to be fruitful and multiply, they were not commanded to multiply after their kind either. What else would they produce? This is to be understood. So we know that the plants also would multiply after their kind without the express statement. Therefore, the command to the earth to bring plants forth "after their kind" must mean after their pre-existing kind.

In the case of the animals, on the fifth day they were created "after their kind," yet not commanded to reproduce after their kind. Again, on the sixth day, it states that God made the animals after their kind, but He does not command them to reproduce after their kind. The reason is the same as that given for the plants. There had been animals before those created during reconstruction week. The existence of animals at the earlier time is proof that plants also existed then; for the animals required food. This is merely a confirmation of what has already been set forth as to pre-existing plants.

Thus an examination of what the Bible actually states regarding plants and animals and what is implied in the context makes it entirely clear that both plants and animals existed on the earth prior to those mentioned in the record of reconstruction week. All of the pre-existing plants and animals were destroyed in a cataclysmic judgment (Gen 1:2) which resulted in the condition mentioned in this same verse. Water finally covered the whole earth and, of course, destroyed everything.

In the light of all this, the consecrated believer in the Bible need not hesitate in the least to accept the confirmatory evidence of science as it is found in the fossils and in other evidence of a physical nature. The fossil evidence of plants and animals in the earth long before man's time is fully convincing. They are found intermingled in every horizon of sedimentary rocks, showing that plants and animals existed together and were destroyed in the past. There is no fossil evidence to the contrary. Thus science supports the Bible.

Was the cataclysm of verse 2 of sufficient magnitude to account for all of the destruction just referred to? This requires consideration. According to the statement given in this verse, the destruction resulted in a world-wide flood accompanied by a corresponding widespread darkness. The water that covered the entire face of the earth necessarily destroyed all animal life in the entire world. The plants perished, at least as food for the animals. All land animals must have perished as they did later at the time of the Deluge. The marine animals must have perished from lack of food and from change in aquatic environment, if not from other causes. The darkness alone would have destroyed all life even if not accompanied by a flood, because light is essential for plant growth. With no plants, there could be no animals either.

The Genesis account seems to mean that the flood and darkness both came upon the earth at the same time; for they are mentioned in the same connection. This being true, they were both the result of a common cause. Even the sun, moon, and stars, and the earth's atmosphere as well, no longer functioned as before. They had to be reconstructed to make the earth habitable. The plants were all destroyed and had to be ordered anew so they would grow again. The animals were all destroyed and had to be created new. Even the created ruler of the earth had to be permanently displaced from his authority; and a new order of being (man) had to be created to rule the earth in his place. (See p. 141.)

This is the profoundest change in the earth that we have any record of. The Deluge caused nothing like this; for in it neither plants, animals nor man were entirely destroyed. None of these forms of life had to be created again afterwards. Hence, the judgment of the Deluge was not sufficiently great to destroy all forms of life. It must have been of lesser violence. Man continued as the ruler of the earth. He was not displaced by a new order of creation. There was no reconstruction of the sun, moon, and stars, nor of the earth's atmosphere. The Deluge did not result in permanent darkness all over the earth, a darkness that had to be dispelled by a special act of God. Plants and animals multiplied after the flood subsided, and this without special pronouncement from God accompanied by a special act of creation.

Certainly, according to the Scriptural account of the two disasters, it was the one previous to man's time that most profoundly affected the earth. And why should not this have been the case? This one was due to the sin of fallen angels, the highest order of created beings. And it was a sin great enough to necessitate judgment. The Deluge was due to judgment because of sin of man, who is a lesser being and therefore not capable of such great consequences. The Deluge merely destroyed the disobedient from the earth, thus freeing the obedient from them and the world that had been before.

Surely a judgment of such consequences as that which resulted from the sin of fallen angels was great enough to account for all of the destruction referred to in the Bible (Gen.1:2a), and for all of the destruction discovered in science. Whether science has yet discovered all of the destruction is very doubtful. Exploration has not yet been carried on long enough to be complete. Of course, much of the evidence is overlooked because of the evolutionary interpretation given in explanation. A speculation disguised as science, and set forth for the purpose of denying or evading judgment as a result of sin, is certain to overlook many of the essential facts. These facts have to be searched out and given their true interpretation.

Extensive fossil beds are found very widely distributed at various horizons from the surface down as far as sedimentary rocks are found. Most of the fossil beds are evidence of life destroyed and buried by some unusual disaster which came with sufficient suddenness to destroy life extensively and bury it deep enough to be preserved. It is not uncommon to find hundreds of small animal fossils in a single cubic yard of rock. The animals are in a perfect state of preservation, thus showing that they were killed and buried suddenly. Fishes are an excellent example of this. Sometimes they are found in a distorted position showing death struggle. They must have died in the convulsion that took place at that time. It killed them and covered them up at the same time.

The objective evidence shows plainly that the entire destruction did not take place at one time. It shows that the destruction was spread over a period of time of unknown duration. There are some reasons for concluding that it was as long as the estimates given for it in the time-table of geology. A very long period of time, it would seem, should be divided into periods. Of course, the time-table has been divided into ages, but this is highly unsatisfactory because the opinions of authorities differ widely. No one attempts to put the matter on a scientific basis. The reason it is so difficult to do so is the impossibility of obtaining sufficient objective data on the conditions that prevailed during the period. Thus far all attempts to do this have been based on evolution. Evolution has never been established. And it never can be established because its assumptions rest on a false foundation. Whether past time previous to man will ever be divided into periods remains to be seen. Thus far, we have found no way of correlation between regions widely separated; without this no progress can be made. Even if we could divide all past time into periods, the question arises, Of what use would it be? The attraction to dividing geological time rests on the support it is said to give to evolution. When evolution is shown to be false, then the superstructure built upon it not only falls, but also is of little further interest.

Near the bottom of the Grand Canyon of the Colorado river in Arizona, there is very definite evidence of faulting and tilting of strata on an extensive scale. The attendant physical destruction must have been very great. Yet all of this disturbed rock is covered by about 4,000 feet of sedimentary rock still in its original horizontal position and barely disturbed at all. The faulting and tilting all took place before the formation above it was deposited.

The faulted and tilted formation must have been exposed as dry land for a long time, because its surface shows much evidence of extensive erosion. This undoubtedly represents a very long time. If we add to this the time required to lay down the 4,000 feet of sedimentary formation and also that required to erode it down to its present surface, then we have the age of the disturbance. We do not know how old the disturbance is. That it is very old is beyond question. It represents disaster at an early time. There is fully established evidence of similar types of disturbances which occurred at various times in other parts of the world also (e.g. Canada, India). If such evidence were not so deeply covered, we should find it much more common.

This shows that there has been a series of phenomena of this kind in different parts of the world in early time. And they were undoubtedly distributed over a long period of time.

There is strong Biblical evidence that the time from primal creation to Adam was very long. Since Lucifer was the highest of created beings, it follows that he received a correspondingly great length of time of probation after he sinned. God's nature is always the same; it should be true that He would show a much greater degree of patience with Satan and the hosts of fallen angels. According to the Bible, there has not been at any time since man was created any hope of redemption held out to fallen angels. In the Bible, Satan is everywhere condemned as an irredeemable sinner. This being true, he must have been condemned at the time of the judgment mentioned in Genesis 1:2. This is spoken of in the Great White Throne Judgment of Revelation 20:11. This judgment will also affect the physical world. It states that the earth and the sun will flee away from the face of God. In fact, the physical world is done away with and a new heaven and a new earth are created (21:1). Hence, sin great enough to result in a final judgment does affect the physical world. It is an awful thing, too horrible for human comprehension. This is no doubt the reason so little is said about it in the Bible. It was not revealed to Adam. He was not aware that it was all implied in the tree of knowledge of good and evil. God did not tell him. All God did was to warn him. Here God placed emphasis upon obedience, not upon a full knowledge of the results of disobedience.

The knowledge of the final judgment of fallen angels has been withheld from man no doubt because it is too awful for him to understand. Perhaps God did not want man to know of the sin of pride which was the downfall of Satan, so that man would not be lured into the same experience through the imaginations of his own heart. He would have to sin on his own and be given the chance not to sin, with no previous example to imitate. His own sin was that of disobedience and finally pride like unto Satan's. We may know some of the details of the physical aspects of judgment, yet we cannot have a full understanding of it. All we can see is some of the effects. The immediate physical cause of these effects is left largely to inference.

The thing we need to know most is that sin is a terrible thing, and that it is to be shunned and its consequences feared as nothing else in the world. This is sufficient understanding for man. Perhaps after he has proved his obedience in the context of what he already knows, he will be trusted with further knowledge.

For the present, man must be satisfied with the knowledge of the fact of the Great Cataclysmic Judgment rather than of its details.

In all probability, Moses (author of Genesis) knew nothing at all about fossils in different parts of the world, not even those where he lived. He was not in communication with the world as we are today. He understood the cataclysmic judgment, however, far better than we would suppose. For he knew God and spoke to Him face to face. He must have had revealed to him some degree of knowledge of the great judgment following primal creation. He must have known its cause and of the need of the reconstruction which had to follow. Surely God's chosen prophet, who was the medium through whom God gave to man the law dealing with sin, must have known the origin and the consequences of the first sin. If there was anything about it that he could not understand as just, he no doubt must have inquired and been enlightened. Otherwise, why should he have had such implicit faith in God's power to deliver Israel from sin as He led them out of Egypt through the wilderness? Surely, we may feel fully convinced that when Moses wrote Genesis, he was informed of the meaning of creation as related to sin.

Even now the truth Moses knew has been discovered only in part. How accurate the account he gives? How sublime the choice of words! Only Divine Inspiration can explain it!

56

V

THE FIRST DAY
(Genesis 1:3-5)

The First Day began with a scene of destruction. An ocean covered the entire surface of the earth. On the surface of the ocean there was universal darkness. The great cataclysm had resulted in a world-wide disaster which left the world incapable of supporting life. Since the world was created to support life, God would not leave it in a ruined condition. Flood and darkness are types of sin. God could not leave the world in such a state permanently, for this would be allowing sin to have the rule over His world that was originally created perfect. It must again support life. In order that it might do so, the ruined world must be reconstructed. Doubtless, reconstruction followed the disaster immediately.

In the accomplishment of this, God's first act was to give the command, "Let there be light." This simple command involves much that is commonly overlooked. Let us consider the most important aspects of it.

It is the first command in the recorded Word. What is the significance of the command? Why should this act be in the form of a command? The first of the recorded acts of God is not connected with a command (Gen.1:1). Why should the creation of the heavens and the earth be without command (Gen. 1:1), whereas this act (Gen.1:3) was in the form of a command? The answer to this is not difficult to find. In God's first act He was bringing the world into existence out of nothing. There had never been in existence anything to oppose His will. All He needed to do was to exercise His own will according to His own desire without hindrance, for no other beings existed, nor was there a physical world. God would not issue a command to Himself.

57

In verse 2, there was no occasion for His command, because the work here recorded was not God's work. "That (Satan) made the world as a wilderness . . . " (Isa. 14:17). It should be noted that God's name is not in any way connected with the second statement of the Bible. In the second sentence of verse 2, it is true that the second one of God's acts is recorded, but the act involved only God Himself. Presumably, it did not affect the physical world. His spirit merely moved (or brooded) over the face of the deep without affecting it, as is recorded. It is in verse 3 that we find for the first time an act of God which affected the physical world. Why did He put His act here in the form of a command? Because He was overcoming one of the results of sin. He was placing in order something that had gone contrary to His will; He was not creating anything new. He was bringing into being order out of disorder. This is the implication of the word let. For example, the expression, "Let me go," implies that the one who gives the command is confined or restrained as to his freedom. The object of the command is to overcome the hindrance.

In the same way, the command, "Let there be light," implies that the light was in existence, but that it was not shining where it should. It implies that there was some hindrance in its way which had to be overcome so the light would shine where it was needed. That the obstacle in the way was not within the will of God is obvious. For if it were in the will of God, then He would be working against Himself in removing it.

The light was commanded to appear in order to dispel the darkness. From this fact alone we should know that the darkness was an evil. In fact, all through the Scriptures darkness is a type of evil. There was darkness all over the land while Jesus hung on the cross (Mat. 27:45). In the Bible there are numerous other examples of darkness as a type of evil.[12] Since darkness is merely the absence of light, we know that darkness did not

---

[12] See Exodus 10:21-23; Joel 3:15.

appear until after light had first been in existence. Otherwise, there would have been no way of producing darkness through the absence of light. Darkness is merely the effect of extinguishing light.

Darkness is the absence of light. It could not be a direct creation in itself. Direct creations are always positive. Darkness is only an effect. All argument that darkness was created before light is wholly wrong. The record of the Bible for the First Day does not state either directly or by implication that light was created at that time. It merely states that light was called into being on the surface of the earth (v. 15). It is impossible to establish the claim that light was created at this time without adding to the Scriptures. This is a thing that no man has a right to do; for it is expressly forbidden.[13] Since we know that light did not first come into existence on the First Day, we know that it was created before this time. After the creation of light, there was also the possibility of darkness when sin entered the world.

The assumption that <u>universal</u> darkness was the condition previous to the beginning (Gen. 1:1) is erroneous. The Bible does not state this anywhere. It merely states that just before the First Day, darkness was upon the face of the deep or waters. It does not state that darkness extended beyond this very limited region of universal space.

"God saw the light that it was good." Calling the light good is equivalent to calling its negative evil. This is obvious, because the light was called into being to dispel the darkness. In all ordinary usage, <u>good</u> is used in opposition to <u>evil</u>. Whenever a thing is called good, the implication is that its antithesis is to be found somewhere for comparison. The thing called good is held in contrast with its opposite, which is held to be evil. If we had no other reason for knowing that sin had been in existence previous to this time, we should easily infer it from this expression (v. 4).

---

[13] Deut. 4:2; Prov. 30:6; Rev. 22:18, 19.

God does nothing without a reason. In the record of His acts in the first chapter, some are designated as good, but others are not so designated. There is a reason in each case. "In the beginning God created the heavens and the earth." No mention is made of the primal creation as good. Obviously not, for it was the only creation in existence. Nothing like it had ever fallen under the influence of sin to be called evil by implication. "And the earth was without form, and void; and darkness was upon the face of the deep." This could not be called good for it was not God's work, and it was evil instead of good. "And the Spirit of God moved upon the face of the waters." This could not be called good, for evidently no change was brought about by it; hence there could be no comparison between good and evil. "And God said, Let there be light: and there was light." Now, for the first time, an act of God brought about a change to overcome an evil condition. This by contrast was called good.

"And God divided the light from the darkness." This is equivalent to saying that He separated the good from the evil. God and evil have nothing in common. They are mutually opposed. The light is a type of Christ, and the darkness is a type of the evil one. "God called the light Day, and the darkness He called Night." Day is also a type of Christ, and Night is a type of the adversary. Why are not these acts of God, dividing light from darkness and naming each, expressly called good? The light was already called good, and by implication the darkness was evil.

"And the evening and the morning were the first day." Here it will be noted that this part of the record is not enumerated with God's stated acts at this time. Neither is it called good. What is the reason for this? Time had been in existence since the beginning (Gen.1:1).[14] Of course, time must have its units of measurement. Day and night, morning and evening had already been in existence, as a consequence of Lucifer's sin. Since God

---

[14] See Chapter III.

had already created the measurement of time, knowing that sin would enter His perfect world, there was no need to mention it as one of His acts at <u>this</u> time. There was no occasion to call this measurement of time good. "In the beginning" (primal creation) there was no different measurement of time with which to compare it.

What kind of light was that which is mentioned on the First Day? Was it sunlight? No, it was not sunlight. The sun was not made to give its light on the earth until the fourth day. The same was true of the moon and the stars. From this fact, we know that the light called into being on the First Day was not natural or created light. The time for the functioning of this kind of light on the surface of the earth did not come until the fourth day. All theorizing on the manner of possible functioning of natural light on the First Day is vain. One theory calls for another to support it, and the whole speculation finally falls. The explanation is not to be found in the theories of man. It is to be found in the Word itself. Let us note in the first place that the light was called Day. It was therefore daylight. But what kind of daylight could there have been before there was sunlight such as we are accustomed to? In the Bible the only kind of light mentioned besides natural light is supernatural light. This is also eternal light. It is mentioned in a number of places. God is clothed with this kind of light. ("Who coverest Thyself with light as with a garment . . ." Ps. 104:2.) After the restoration is complete and all sin is done away with, this eternal light from God and the Lamb shall become the light of the new heaven and the new earth. Then there will be no natural light at all. For the sun and the moon and the light of the candle will be done away with. (See Rev. 21:23, 25; 22:5.) "God is light, and in Him is no darkness at all." (I John 1:5.) Sin is darkness, and it is separation from God.

Consequently, we know that the darkness with which the First Day began was evil; it meant separation from God. He will finally dispel all darkness with His own eternal light. Hence, we may reasonably infer that the first light He called into being to take the place of the darkness on the First Day was also this same light. He made it to function for three days until it was displaced by natural light on the fourth day. Thus, the world of sin began its reconstruction temporarily with eternal light as a type of that which would finally conquer all darkness and sin.

The eternal light was everywhere present and needed only God's will to cause it to appear. He did not shed this light permanently on everything in the world. He had it shine continuously only for the day. The night was left dark as the type of evil. God was not at this time creating the new heaven and the new earth that will stand forever. The world of this time was only the temporal world in which man would sin in due time, thus rendering the world imperfect again.

The events of the First Day are named in succession, beginning with the command, "Let there be light," and ending with naming the darkness Night. These events took place during a period of time constituting one literal day made up of an evening or night, and a morning or daylight. The fact that it was made up of an evening and a morning is evidence that it was a literal day, because among the Hebrews this was the customary way of dividing the day. The literal day with Hebrews begins at sunset. Its first half is composed of the evening called night, and this is followed by the second half called morning or sometimes day, as distinguished from night. This custom of reckoning the day from sunset to sunset is still followed by many orthodox Hebrews.

One of the absurd and foolish claims made in modern higher education is that the days mentioned in the first chapter of Genesis are aeons of unmeasured duration with no definite beginning or end. This foolish idea never gained a hearing until evolution became prominent in the twentieth century. It is the natural outcome of the subjective method of reading the Bible. Those who read the Bible in this manner read their own ideas into it without regard for its authority as divinely inspired. How their view upholds the authority of the Bible and honors God they never seek to show. Occasionally, "Hebrew scholarship" is used feebly to uphold the idea that a day means an aeon. The difficulties involved in the Hebrew language, however, are just the same as they are in the English translation. The principle is the same. In any language a book of authority must say what it means and not something else.

The Command, LET

Let is a command. It is an order issued against something that is not as the one giving the command desires it to be. The execution of the command implies something to be done by a power external to the one issuing the command. It always implies an opposing force or power to be overcome in some manner.

In the record of creation and reconstruction the word let occurs only on the six days. It is not used in any way in connection with God's act of rest on the seventh day, nor in connection with His act of blessing and sanctifying the day after it had passed, nor in the original act of creation (Gen. 1:1).

The word occurs as follows: (1) "Let there be light" (v.3). (2) "Let there be a firmament in the midst of the waters (v.6). (3) "Let it divide the waters from the waters" (v.6). (4) "Let the waters under the heaven be gathered unto one place" (v.9). (5) "Let the dry land appear" (v.9). (6) "Let the earth bring forth grass . . . and the tree yielding fruit" (v.11). (7) "Let there be lights in the firmament of the heaven to divide the day from the night" (v.14). (8) "Let them be for signs, and for days, and for years" (v. 14). (9) "Let them be for lights in the firmament of the heaven to give light upon the earth" (v.15). (10) "Let the waters bring forth abundantly the moving creature that hath life" (v.20). (11) "Let fowl multiply upon the earth" (v.22). (12) "Let the earth bring forth the living creature after his kind" (v.24). (13) "Let us make man after our image, after our likeness" (v.26). (14) "Let them have dominion over the fish of the sea, and over the fowl of the air, and over the cattle, and over all the earth" (v.26).

63

Why were these fourteen commands given? (1) That there might be light instead of darkness. (2) That there might be a firmament in the midst of the waters, instead of a state of confusion. (3) That the firmament might divide the waters instead of there being a state of confused intermingling of waters above and below. (4) That the waters (seas) under the heavens might be gathered into one place instead of flooding everything. (5) That the dry land might appear instead of remaining submerged by the flood of the destruction. (6) That the earth might bring forth plants instead of remaining nonproductive and in ruin. (7) That there might be lights in the firmament of heaven to divide the day from the night in order that life might be supported instead of being destroyed by constant darkness. (8) That the lights might be for signs, and for seasons, and for days, and for years, instead of there being a state of dateless confusion. (9) That these lights might give light upon the earth, instead of merely giving light unto the expanse above the earth. (10) That the water might bring forth animal life, instead of being merely a scene of ruin. (11) That the fowl might be re-created to multiply upon the earth, instead of remaining destroyed. (12) That the earth might bring forth every kind of animal life, instead of remaining destroyed. (13) That the earth might have in it a being made after the image of God, instead of remaining destroyed by the sin of the one who did not bear God's image. (14) That the newly created man might rule all the earth, instead of allowing it to remain without a ruler who would do God's will.

For the fourteen commands these are the reasons as revealed directly or as implied in the record. Each command begins with <u>let</u>. Each one was for the definite purpose of establishing order instead of the ruin and confusion that had prevailed. In each case something not in accord with God's will was put in order by divine command against the disorder. It was a sorrow to Him to have to do this, because He is always grieved over sin and its consequences.

In contrast with this it should be noted that the original creation recorded in Gen. 1:1 does not begin with a command of any kind. Nor does the command beginning with let occur in connection with the sentence, "And the evening and the morning were the first day." The division of the literal day into day and night had just been accomplished through a command beginning with let, and there was left only one more thing to do and that was to record the length of time involved in the series of events beginning with "Let there be light," and ending with, "And God called the light Day and the darkness He called Night." The text does not state that the day with its evening and the morning was created here. It merely states that the evening and the morning, as just previously named, were, or constituted, the First Day. The term day appears in the account without introduction: thus we may assume that the day had already been in existence.

No command of any kind is given in connection with God's resting on the seventh day, nor with sanctifying it. These acts of His did not involve anything outside of Himself. There was nothing to oppose His will in connection with these two acts.

The events of the First day were:

(a) "God said, Let there be light."
(b) "And there was light."
(c) "God saw that the light was good."
(d) "God called the light Day, and the darkness Night."

No details are mentioned in connection with any of the four events. They were all instantaneous; hence, without details. Yet, they were distributed over a period of one day composed of an evening (night) and a morning (daylight).

The succession of night and day which continued through the days that followed signifies that sin continued to exist in the world. And this has been true ever since. It will continue to be true as long as sin exists, which will be until after the Great White Throne Judgment (Rev. 20:11). When sin is done away with, then the succession of night and day will cease. "And there shall be no night there; and they need no candle, neither light of the sun; for the Lord God giveth them light; and they shall reign for ever and ever." (Rev. 22:5.)

VI

THE SECOND DAY
(Genesis 1:6-8)

The first day had to do with light and darkness called Day and Night. The recording of these two periods is in the reverse order for us: "And the <u>evening</u> and the <u>morning</u> were the first day." There is a reason for everything God does. The disrupted earth which He was about to put in order was lying in a state of darkness typical of the sin which caused it. God had to begin the reconstruction in a world of darkness and sin. Out of this He was to bring forth light and righteousness. Hence, the literal day which signified righteousness was made to begin with darkness or night and to end with the light or day called morning. Othodox Hebrews, as we noted, still adhere to Genesis by beginning the day at sunset.

Having established light, day and night, evening and morning for the first day, God next turned His attention to the firmament above the ocean, which still covered the whole earth. The firmament was simply the atmosphere. We may know this from the record of the fifth day (v. 20), where it states that the fowl were "to fly above the earth in the open firmament of heaven." It is sometimes called <u>the</u> <u>expanse</u>.

The firmament was commanded into existence in a new form on the Second Day. Opposition to God's will is sin or the consequence of sin. The state of the firmament at this time was a result of the great cataclysmic judgment of verse 2. It appears to have been an intermingling of the waters in the form of water vapor and mist. This was what shut out from the earth the light of the sun and the other heavenly bodies. The nature of the cataclysm may be inferred in part from this. It was a disaster of such proportions as to defy our imagination.

67

"And God made (not created) the firmament, and divided the waters which were under the firmament from the waters which were above the firmament; and it was so" (v.7). The waters under it we may easily understand to be the ocean. Concerning the waters above it we may not be so certain, because there is nothing to correspond with that condition now. We must, however, bear in mind that the Flood of Noah's time has taken place since to alter atmospheric conditions.

The language used in this verse indicates an atmosphere highly charged with water vapor. Liquid water is hardly to be understood from the expression "waters above the firmament." Could liquid waters exist above the firmament or atmosphere? This we are not told. We are left entirely to inference, guided only by our present imperfect knowledge of science and by the Scriptural record concerning the Flood. (See Job 36:27, 38:37.)

It is observed that of the acts of God on the Second Day there is no immediate pronouncement of good for any of them. Of the several acts mentioned, only one involved a constructive act regarding the physical world. It pertained to the firmament. It is stated that God made it. Hence, this act would be included in the general pronouncement of good, made at the close of the sixth day where it is stated, "And God saw everything that He had made, and behold, it was very good" (v.31).

"And God called the firmament Heaven." This was, of course, atmospheric heaven or "the expanse." This is also called the first heaven, as distinguished from the second or starry heaven, and as distinguished from the third heaven, or the heaven of heavens, where God dwells. A failure to make this distinction leads to confusion in understanding the Scriptures involved.

"And the evening and the morning were the second day." Here, as in each of the other days, the evening and the morning constituted, as we've shown, the literal day.

In the account of the firmament or atmosphere of the Second Day, it will be observed that the firmament is not divided into climatic zones as is the atmosphere of the present. The atmosphere is spoken of as a unit. There were no desert climates, no semiarid climates, nor were there frigid and torrid climates. Because none of the climates of the present time is ideal for life, they could not have existed at the close of the Second Day; for the atmosphere was put in ideal condition for the living. It was to function perfectly, not imperfectly as at present.

Climate is an obvious result of atmospheric conditions. An ideal climate requires an ideal atmosphere. The ideal climate is one perfectly adapted to the support of life, both plant and animal, as well as human. Life at present is so imperfect that it is very difficult to determine from its present state just what were the conditions for its ideal state at the beginning.

At least this much is obvious: That the temperature was mild rather than torrid or frigid; and that it was not a combination of both, as is the case with our so-called "temperate" climate of the present. We can know this from the fact that a mild temperature is best for both plant and animal life. It is also the best suited for man's comfort. In a unified climatic world such as existed at the chose of the Second Day the conditions favorable for one form of life were also favorable for all forms of life.

Man was the highest form of life to occupy the newly reconstructed world. We may judge from him what were the ideal conditions for the other forms of life. He lived in this atmosphere unclad and, of course, in perfect comfort. At present the optimum temperature for man as clad is about 68° F. From this, we infer that the first man may have required a temperature 20° to 30° higher. The humidity requisite for comfort is 60 per cent to 75 per cent. It may not have been very much different from this in the beginning. With higher humidity and other conditions no longer existing, the atmosphere filtered out injurious rays from the sun which now cause harm to life.

From this we may conclude that there was but little variation from the above named temperature and humidity in any part of the world. Plant and animal life must have been perfectly adapted to this condition. Indeed, plants and animals still thrive best under this condition, except such forms as have been modified (to make minor changes) to meet adverse conditions which have since arisen. The animals of our time have been subject to modification and decline because of the toll that sin has made on the physical body. Many that we call different species today are only varieties. (See Chapter XIV.)

Under these conditions everywhere prevalent in the atmosphere, there were no winds in any part of the world. The wind zones of the present climate are due to the widely divergent temperatures between the equatorial belt and the polar areas. The polar areas maintain an average temperature fully 100° F. below that of the equatorial belt. These two extremes give rise to a permanent circulation of air between them, which accounts for the permanent wind zones. With a uniform temperature all over the world, the condition necessary for the circulation between the wind zones could not exist. Winds are an effect. With their cause wanting, there could be no winds. Winds are not mentioned until after the Flood.

Under the present atmospheric conditions resulting in the very unequal distribution of heat and moisture, we have violent destructive storms such as tornadoes in the temperate climatic regions and hurricanes and typhoons in the torrid climatic zone. Under a uniform climate of mild temperature and humidity, none of these and other storms would be possible. Storms are unnatural. Animals seek shelter from them. Man does not enjoy them either.

An atmosphere highly charged with water vapor is the most effective thermal blanket. This was the condition of the Second Day. The heat of the sun was held in the atmosphere by this thermal blanket instead of being radiated out into space as at present. Hence, there was but little range in the daily and annual temperature. This is in striking contrast with present conditions. As evidence that moisture in the air renders the air a more effective thermal blanket resulting in very little daily and annual range of temperature, we need only observe that as a result of cloudiness the moisture content of the air is high all day and all night, and the daily variation of temperature is slight—frequently less than five degrees, not enough to affect our comfort.

It should not be concluded for this reason, however, that the reconstructed atmosphere was one constantly overcast. Such an atmosphere would not be favorable for life, because life requires more light than is afforded by an overcast sky. Hence, the atmosphere must have been clear enough to permit the free passage of light through it.

Were there clouds in the atmosphere of the Second Day? There could not have been clouds such as result in storms, for the reasons given above. Nor could there have been clouds that give rise to lightning, for lightning is destructive. This condition could not have existed in a perfect world with everything co-ordinated. The effectiveness of the air as a thermal blanket was due to the water vapor present rather than to the clouds as such. Water vapor is transparent and may be present in large amounts without condensation to form clouds.

Clouds are in part a result of dust particles in the air. Dust particles serve as nuclei around which the water vapor condenses to form the droplets which make up a cloud. Without these dust particles, there would be no droplets and as a result no clouds.

We are so accustomed to dust in the air that we naturally assume that this condition has always existed. Let us, however, consider the nature and origin of dust that we may be able to judge whether dust has always been in the air. Most of the dust is made up of fine particles of soil which have become dried out, then carried forth by the winds. By far the greater portion of the dust comes from the deserts. As more than half of the land surface is arid or semiarid, it is easy to understand where the constant supply of atmospheric dust comes from. Another source of dust is from volcanic eruptions of the explosive type. These have been known to throw enough dust into the air to be carried several times around the world in the course of several years. Smoke, bacteria, and plant spores are minor sources of dust. Smoke did not exist in the beginning. Bacteria as known to us may not have existed either, for they appear to be a form of perversion of nature. Plant spores could not have found their way into the higher atmosphere without winds to carry them. They must have been confined to the lower atmosphere where they were needed to serve their purpose (reproduction).

Dust from volcanoes, deserts, and forms of perverted life is a pollution. Such a condition is inconsistent with an atmosphere reconstructed by the act of God. The atmosphere which He made must have been pure and, therefore, free from dust that would cause clouds. In our time clouds form everywhere, and even in altitudes as high as nine miles or more.

Hence, we should conclude that the atmosphere at the close of the Second Day was free from dust and also free from clouds such as we have at the present time. It would also be true that there would be no twilight period just after sunset or just before sunrise. The change from night to day in the morning and also from day to night in the evening would have been sudden instead of gradual. Night would not be as dark as it is under present conditions. The sky would always be clear, and there would be no obstruction to the passage of light through it. Shadows would be more clearly defined also. With an atmosphere free from dust, the world would be far more beautiful than it is.

Further knowledge of the atmospheric conditions at the close of the Second Day is found by making the conditions that existed just after the Flood a basis of comparison. "While the earth remaineth, seedtime and harvest, and cold and heat, and summer and winter, and day and night shall not cease." (Gen. 8:22.) These words contain the very first mention of climatic conditions bearing a resemblance to those of the present. Yet even this account does not state that the seasons were not at that time as severe as they are now. Consider the context. As soon as Noah went out of the ark, he built an altar unto the Lord and offered burnt offerings. Following the example of Abel (Gen. 4:4), it was pleasing unto the Lord (Gen. 8:21). And the Lord said in His heart that He would not again curse the ground for man's sake; and He also added regarding seedtime and harvest, cold and heat, summer and winter, that they would not cease "while the earth remaineth" (v. 22).

Because God was pleased with Noah's offerings, He gave Noah favorable climatic conditions for a continuation of the offerings. Furthermore, God blessed Noah and his sons and commanded them to "be fruitful, and multiply, and replenish the earth." (Gen. 9:1.) A blessing carries with it joy. From this we can know that the climate was in keeping with man's comfort. The command to replenish the earth did not exclude any portion of the earth; hence, the climate was favorable everywhere. This is confirmed in the further command to "bring forth abundantly in the earth, and multiply therein" (v. 7).

In establishing His covenant with Noah, God extended it also to the animals (Gen. 8:21)—further evidence of a favorable climate everywhere. It is clear that God would not give the command to fill the earth with people and with animals and confirm it with a covenant without at the same time providing fully for carrying out His command. Hence, we know that the present climate did not exist at the time the command was given. God could not give a command and at the same time place an obstacle in the way, making it impossible to carry out the command.

That the climate was mild after the Flood in regions where it is now very severe is confirmed by fossil evidence. The mastodons[15] found frozen in the ice of northern Siberia are a good example of this. The flesh is still preserved so well that dogs will eat it. The skin is also well preserved. Undigested food is found in the stomach, also well preserved.

Since the mastodon lived only in a mild climate, we know that northern Siberia had such a climate at the time these animals were there. The fact that they are found frozen in the ice, but well preserved, is proof that they were caught in a sudden blizzard. It proves also that the cold remained severe

---

[15] Extinct mammal, "elephant".

continuously to the present time, otherwise the flesh would not still be preserved. We know also that this occurred <u>since</u> the Flood; otherwise the Flood waters would have melted the ice from the animal body, and decay would have resulted.

That the sudden cold did not occur immediately after the Flood is clear from the Genesis account as set forth above. Although we know that the cold set in after the Flood, we do not know just how soon this occurred. Nor do we know how general were the conditions which prevailed in northern Siberia. The evidence is that the cold set in within the first several centuries following the Flood. This cold climate followed the spread of sin when man got away from the vivid memory of the Flood as a judgment. In our own time man has gotten so far away from it as to deny the Flood altogether.

Although the climate immediately following the Flood was much more ideal than that of the present, it is nevertheless far inferior to that of reconstruction week. By the time of the Flood, the world had suffered under more than sixteen centuries of sin, and sin always carries with it some measure of the first curse (Gen. 3:17, 19). It affects man's work of making a living through toil.

The seasons instituted at the time of the creation of man were ideal in all respects, perfectly suited to man's well-being. Variations of the seasons were necessarily within the limits of man's comfort. As the dispensations under sin advanced, the extremes affecting man's well-being gradually increased.

At the close of the Second Day, climatic conditions were perfectly suited to the support of life; for on the day following, plants were ordered as soon as the land appeared above the sea. With the further provision for sunlight, moonlight, and the light of the stars, conditions were designed for animals and for man. This was to be completed on the fourth day.

The events of the Second-Day were:

(a) "God said, Let there be a firmament in the midst of the water."

(b) "And let it divide the waters from the waters."

(c) "God made the firmament."

(d) "And divided the waters which were under the firmament from the waters that were above the firmament."

(e) "And it was so."

(f) "And God called the firmament Heaven."

These events were distributed over a period of an evening and a morning, which constituted the Second Day.

The purpose of the work of the Second Day was to reconstruct the atmosphere so it would function favorably for the support of life. It had to be put into condition to permit the passage of natural light; for this kind of light was to be in effect on the second day following.

The condition existing previously was not in keeping with His will; otherwise, He would not have reconstructed anything. Therefore, the previous condition was not His own work, but the work of an enemy. It was necessary for God to reconstruct this in order to assert His power over the enemy.

What natural phenomena were connected with this work of the enemy to produce the condition mentioned in verse 2? The darkness mentioned in this verse was due to an atmospheric condition which prevented the sunlight from reaching the surface of the earth. If this had not been the case, there would have been no need of calling forth light to dispel the darkness, as was done on the first day, nor of reconstructing the atmosphere (firmament), as was done on the Second Day. The darkness must have been due to a dense fog over all the earth. Condensation of moisture due to lowering of the temperature of the air was probably the natural means by which this was caused.

The lowering of the temperature after the Flood (Deluge), however, may be understood by considering the conditions prevailing at that time. The atmosphere had lost much of its water vapor ("And the rain was upon the earth forty days and forty nights." Gen.7:12), yet not all of it. ("The fountains also of the deep and the windows of heaven were stopped, and the rain from heaven was restrained" Gen. 8:2.) For this reason, the atmosphere was a less perfect thermal blanket than it had been, and, of course, it began to cool off in the regions where it received the least solar heat, which was at the poles. As this process continued, the freezing temperature was reached in time, and then the precipitation was in the form of snow. At this stage the difference in temperature between the polar and the equatorial regions caused a circulation of winds between the two extremes of temperature on the same principle as prevails at present.

This circulation carried large amounts of moisture to the polar regions, where, in time, it became stored up in the form of snow and ice at temperatures not much below freezing. This, in fact, is the temperature at which the heaviest snowfalls occur even at the present time. It began first at the poles and later at lesser latitudes. The snows were distributed to some extent according to the direction of the prevailing winds, which must have blown mainly from the north.

This is the way the Ice Age was brought on with its relatively mild climate at first, gradually changing to the climate of the present time. The evidence found in the Bible and supported by many facts observed on the earth leads to the conclusion that immediately after the Flood a mild, tropical climate prevailed all over the world. Hence, tropical life spread in the higher latitudes and flourished there. As the cooling process continued, the snows extended farther from the poles and the accompanying winds brought the cold suddenly to the marginal regions. In this way tropical animals were caught in latitudes as high as that of north Siberia.

In the middle and higher latitudes, after the atmosphere became depleted of its moisture, it became a much less effective thermal blanket. This resulted in the climate of the present in these latitudes, one of great extremes and sudden changes.

A mild climate in high latitudes is so very different from that which prevails at present that it appears impossible. Some have tried to account for the change in climate by assuming a shift in the position of the axis of the earth. This, however, does not explain it; for even during the present polar summer, which is the most favorable, the climate is still far colder than that of the tropics. Not only is the atmosphere the thermal blanket of the earth, but the equalizer and distributor of the heat which is received from the sun as well. A rare (thin) atmosphere does this imperfectly, as at present in high altitudes. A dense atmosphere highly charged with water vapor as on the Second Day and until after the Flood would do this perfectly.

These conclusions will be evident to anyone who takes the pains to familiarize himself with the principles of meteorology as they have been worked out in recent years. Because of insufficient data, science alone is not sufficient to give the explanation of the great change in climate. If, however, the facts given in the Bible be taken into consideration also, it becomes clear.

What has just been set forth regarding the present atmosphere pertains to its lower portion, the layer next to the earth. This is a region of striking variation in temperature, resulting in winds, clouds, and storms, and the attendant phenomena called weather. This region, called the troposphere, extends to an average elevation of about seven miles.

The upper atmosphere or portion at altitudes greater than this is of fairly constant temperature; and it maintains its uniformity independent of the latitude. There are, of course, no winds, no clouds, and no storms in this region. It is called the stratosphere.

In the lower region of the stratosphere there has been sufficient exploration to prove that the temperature rises slowly with increased altitude, and that this does not vary with the latitude. In the light of recent discoveries, the temperature rises still more with increased altitude until, at an altitude of about 60 miles (mesosphere), it is comparable to that of the tropics on the surface of the earth at sea level (100° F).[16] In the troposphere, the layer next to the earth's surface, the atmosphere is divided into climatic zones that for the most part are not favorable to life.

The recent discoveries regarding the upper atmosphere referred to are in keeping with the conclusion based on purely Biblical evidence that previous to the Flood the atmosphere was ideal everywhere on the surface of the earth and also even to great altitudes. Our conclusion is that if the water vapor that was precipitated in the form of rain at the time of the Flood were returned to the atmosphere, we should again have an ideal climate. Even if the atmosphere were only partly restored, it would be more ideal. It would again rain in the deserts. Man's tenure of life would be increased. Now it is only about 1/20 of what it was before the Flood. Much of this will be realized during the Millennium.

Fact: 90% of the world's population today live at altitudes of less than two thousand feet because atmospheric pressure affects man's comfort and his well-being. God would not call forth areas of dry land of high altitude and low atmospheric pressure, and then three days later create man not at all suited to it.

---

[16] See EARTH, Raymond Siever (San Francisco: W.H. Freeman and Co., 1985) p. 343, Figure 13-4.

VII

THE THIRD DAY
(Genesis 1:9-13)

"And God said, Let the waters under the heaven be gathered unto one place, and let the dry land appear: and it was so."

The condition of the waters or ocean and of the land under the atmospheric heaven at the beginning of the Third Day was not in accord with the will of God. This is implied in the command of reconstruction beginning with the word let, as already explained. As the purpose of the land and the water is that of supporting life—though of different kinds—a reconstruction was necessary before life could exist.

We should note that neither the word make nor create appears in the record given here. Nothing was created, everything was commanded into position. The waters were gathered unto one place instead of being everywhere. The dry land was commanded to appear, obviously raised from beneath the sea. Since the waters were gathered unto one place, it naturally follows that the land occupied the remaining place. From this we conclude that the land was all in one body and the waters likewise. In this way the entire land body was readily available for the migration of life. This was a necessity in a unified world such as God would reconstruct. The land of our own time is one divided into districts. This has been caused by sin. (Gen. 11:1-9.)

The land appeared as dry land. We are not to suppose that the land of this time was like that of the present time. The land of the present is in a widely varying condition. It supports a wide variety of life which is far from ideal. Most of the land is too dry. Some of it is too wet. None of it is ideal. Neither the desert nor the swamp could have existed in the reconstruction, because they would not have served the purpose of supporting

79

life in the best way. Besides, it is called simply "dry land." It is all designated by the same term. Hence, it must have been essentially the same.

It is not designated as rock, gravel, sand, and soil, as we should have to designate it in our time. Nor is it designated as plateaus and mountains or hills. Such land forms cannot be understood here without adding to the Word and without introducing confusion into the world. Bare rock does not support life. It must be made into soil first. God would not bring forth rock when He needed soil to serve His purpose. To claim that He made the rock here and then allowed it to weather away to form soil is wholly wrong; for the plants requiring soil were to be called into being on the very same day. A land area that is partly rock is not in a condition to function perfectly. It could not serve its purpose until after the lapse of much time. This would introduce the element of evolution in the world even before sin had entered it. It would mean that the omnipotent Creator was sharing His power with His creature, as if He did not Himself have power to accomplish His purpose at once. Evolution has no place in creation or in reconstruction.

All of the rugged relief features due to erosion require time for their formation. They are due to weathering. This is caused chiefly by freezing, thawing, rain, and other climatic changes during a long period of time. It is impossible, of course, to account for them through divine decree, because they are not adapted for supporting life in the most favorable way.

Were there any mountains at that time to ornament the landscape as they do now? No, there is no reason for supposing that mountains or even hills existed. Rugged formations of this type are usually mostly rock or some other feature not well suited to supporting life. They are obstacles to life, both for its support of life and for its migration from place to place.

Mountains are an obstacle to life from the standpoint of temperature also. Under present weather conditions, the temperature falls rapidly with increase in altitude. As a result, most mountain ranges are practically waste land. Of course, we have no way of knowing how rapidly the temperature fell with increase in altitude under the atmospheric conditions of the Third Day. Under any condition the difference in temperature must have been considerable, certainly enough to offer a climate hostile to life. Mountains and high hills are always an obstacle to plants and thus, indirectly, also an obstacle to animals. This would make mountains an obstacle to man also, for man is dependent upon plants for his food. Since man was created to have dominion over the animals, they must be able to live in his environment.

Were not the mountains necessary to add to the beauty of the world? Some say this must surely be true, because mountains figure so very prominently in art. Such remarks are often heard. Yet those who say they love the mountains for their beauty never claim that their admiration is based on anything else than merely seeing them. They like to look at mountains from a distance especially. But they have no desire at all to be compelled to make a living in the places that are regarded as the most scenic. Yet, usually the more scenic a place is, the less desirable it is as a place to live.

The standard of beauty ascribed to mountains is not a Scriptural one at all. The Bible nowhere speaks of the mountains as beautiful, nor as coming from God in a perfect world. They are usually spoken of in connection with sin, either expressed or implied. In fact, mountains and high hills are nowhere mentioned in the Bible until the time of the Deluge. It is significant that they are first mentioned in connection with the first judgment of man that fell upon the world because of sin (Gen. 8:4). The "high places" became shrines to immorality in Canaan by those idolatrous nations. The Israelites were commanded to destroy them when they entered the lands of the heathen. When Israel herself tried to worship the true God in such places but with idolatrous symbols, these places were denounced by the prophets. God's judgment fell time and time again upon them because of it. "And they built the high places of Baal . . . Molech . . .; which I commanded them not, neither came it into my mind," saith the Lord God (Jer. 32:35).

The strength and majesty and endurance of the mountains sometimes reminded them of their all-powerful God and brought them comfort as they would look toward the "hills" while in exile, knowing that their strength and help came from Him. (Ps. 121.) Mt. Zion was such a <u>hill</u>, referred to as Jehovah's place, and the place of His sanctuary (Joel 3:17; Psalm 84).

Isaiah says, "How beautiful upon the mountains are the feet of him that bringeth good tidings, that publisheth peace." (Isa. 52:7.) This passage does not state that the mountains are beautiful, but the feet of him that bringeth good tidings. It would seem that the reason this messenger of salvation is made to stand upon the mountain is to show the striking contrast between the message of peace with its salvation, and the message of strife and disruption due to sin which is found typified in the mountains. It is significant to note that the inspired account of the crucifixion of the Savior includes in the record the fact that He was crucified upon a rocky hill (Calvary). (Luke 22:33.) It is also stated that at the beginning of His ministry Satan took Him up into a high mountain to be tempted. (Isaiah 40:3.)

The idea of the beauty of mountains as expressed in art is of mere human origin. The standards of secular art are human all the way through and vary with the times in which they are produced.

Thus, the dry land that was made to appear by divine command was simply land ideally suited to support life. It was fertile soil and doubtless soil of great depth, perhaps similar to that found today in our most fertile areas in the tropics. Its altitude is not stated; but from the expression "dry land," we may infer that it was of sufficient elevation to be well drained, not so low as to be undrained and swampy, or so high as to be too cold and poorly watered. It was such land as was ideal for life at its highest efficiency. This conception honors God by attributing to Him the power and the wisdom to make an ideal place for life. The other conception which assumes relief features like those of the present time does violence to the Scriptures and dishonors God. It tends to exalt the speculation of man and to give them a dignity beyond their merit.

"And God called the dry land Earth; and the gathering together of the waters He called Seas: and God saw that it was good." If the dry land had been rock or other barren formation, it would not have been called Earth; it would have been named accordingly. Soil is sometimes called Earth, but it is never called rock. Mountains are not made of soil; they are made of rock and usually a very rugged and useless form of it.

The gathering together of the waters was called Seas. One simple term for it all, for it was all alike. God's words are always simple and easily understood when taken as they are written. It is when man's speculations are added that the matter becomes complex and hard to understand.

Finally, when the ordering and the naming of the land and the sea were completed, "God saw that it was good." Why should this be a part of the record? God, who never does anything in vain, had a reason for recording these words. It was good because of the contrast with their former condition which was evil as a result of sin. Dry land above the sea is good in contrast with land that was beneath the sea because of a destructive flood. And looking to the future, it was good because it was perfectly suited to the purpose for which it was brought forth—to support life abundantly. If it had been only partly adapted to the support of life, as is the case with the world today, it would not have been possible for God to call it good, because He does not speak as man does. When He calls anything good, it is really and completely so, not relatively so in the sense that man speaks of things.

Man calls anything good that he considers suited to his needs in his own world. In his eagerness to avail himself of the benefit of what he regards good, he loses sight of the inherent evil that lies behind the good; and in his disregard of the evil he overlooks the source of evil, which is the Evil One. He takes the good for granted and thus overlooks the Giver of all good, who is God.

83

When the land and seas were put into condition for sustaining life, God immediately brought forth life by the following command, "And God said, Let the earth bring forth grass, the herb yielding seed, and the fruit tree yielding fruit after his kind, whose seed is in itself, upon the earth: and it was so." Nothing was created. The earth was merely commanded to bring forth the plants, and plants were made, as definitely stated in Genesis 2:4, 5. In Exodus 20:11, the making of the plants is also plainly implied. Since the earth was commanded and plants were made or refashioned at this time, it follows that they had been in existence before. The destruction of the great cataclysm did not fully destroy them. We are justified in concluding that though the plants themselves were destroyed, their seeds were not destroyed. We know that seeds are preserved a long time in water. At the time of the Flood of Genesis 7, the plants were not taken into the ark for their preservation, nor were they re-created afterward. So they must have sprung up from the seeds or from the roots after the Flood. Likewise, in the great destruction recorded in verse 2, the plants had to pass through a flood much in the same way as they did later at the time of the Deluge; and they must have been preserved through their seeds and roots in the same way. The water evidently did not cover all the earth long enough to destroy the plants entirely (Gen. 1:2). Reconstruction must have followed very soon.

Since the former plants were not entirely destroyed, it may be asked, Why were not the plants allowed to spring forth naturally from the seeds and roots just as they do today upon recently drained ground? There are several reasons why this course was not followed. It would have required time. Such plants as full grown trees require many years to reach maturity. Even the fruits and seeds need months to mature. Here, just three days later, man would need fruit as food and full-grown trees for his comfort. And the animals would require food on the second day following, as well as full-grown trees for shade and shelter. These are reasons why the first plants were not called forth through natural generation.

The animals would have for food every green herb; and the man would have the seed and the fruit of every plant except one for his food. From this it follows that there were to be no poisonous plants in the newly reconstructed world. That poisonous plants were among those that were destroyed in the great cataclysm is abundantly confirmed by the fossil record found in the rocks. Their presence is explained by the fact that, following their perfect creation in the beginning, they came under the influence of sin that finally resulted in the cataclysmic judgment. This subject is treated more fully in Chapter IV.

If the plants of God's original creation, now affected through the curse of sin, had been allowed to spring up by natural propagation on the Third Day, the poisonous varieties would have been propagated with the others. This would not have been in keeping with the world that God was now bringing into being. God commanded the earth, therefore, to bring forth the plants He desired. Whether He allowed the evil plants to be destroyed, or whether He cleansed them from their poisons, we cannot know. Furthermore, God would not have honored Himself by calling evil plants into being, or by calling evil plants good. Hence, we know that He did not do so.

As soon as the command was given to the earth to bring forth the plants as mentioned, it came to pass. The plants that appeared are called <u>grass</u>, and <u>herb</u> and <u>tree</u>. They are not called the blade of the grass, nor the leaf of the herb, nor the seedling of the tree. The plants were made to spring forth in full maturity. This was God's way of calling into being the first plants of the reconstruction. Their successors were brought forth by natural generation, just as is the case at the present time.

With the first plants, it was a case of the infinite producing the finite. It required no time. But for the production of succeeding plants by natural generation, the finite produces the finite by natural law, which requires time, as is abundantly clear from observation. The principle of the infinite producing the finite is the same as in the miracles of the Son recorded in the New Testament, as when He fed the five thousand with five barley loaves and two fishes. It did not require time for Him to bring into being the additional food needed to feed the multitude.

The plants all sprang forth yielding fruit and seed after their kind of species, as they were created to do in the first place. The record does not state that any new species of plants were created at this time. If they had been created at this time, the expression "yielding seed after its kind" would not be used. It would be superfluous; for in a world of law and order such as was now being brought forth, every plant and every animal as well would of necessity have to reproduce after its kind; otherwise, the world would come to confusion and life would cease. The implication that plants and animals direct from the perfect hand of God would not reproduce after their kind is a reflection upon Him, and He could not record such a thing in His Word. Yet He does record the expression "after its kind" here to signify that He was not creating new species at this time and also to imply that He had created the species in the beginning.

These plants were pronounced good because they were free from the imperfections of the ones destroyed and, therefore, perfectly suited for their purpose, that of furnishing food and comfort for man and beast. Plants such as these, in comparison with the ones that had been ruined by the judgment, could be called good.

The expression "And God saw that it was good" is used twice in the record of the Third Day. This is because two phases of reconstruction took place, that of land and water and that of the plants. Each was a restoration of what had been destroyed and also a preparation for what was to follow.

VIII

THE FOURTH DAY
(Genesis 1:14-19)

The light that had been functioning since the first day was not from the sun, moon, and stars. These sources of light are mentioned for the first time on the Fourth Day. They had been in existence from the beginning of creation, but from the great cataclysmic judgment until the Fourth Day they were not giving their light upon the earth. We assume that this was due partly to imperfect atmospheric conditions and partly to the sun, moon, and stars not being in the right position in space to shed sufficient light upon the earth. This implies, of course, that they were thrown out of their position in connection with the cataclysmic judgment of verse 2. The most obvious inference is that both of these conditions of disorder prevailed at the close of this great judgment. That the atmosphere was affected in such a manner that it shut out the light is plainly inferred from statements in Genesis, as already explained.

That the heavenly lights were not in the right position in space to shed their light upon the earth, however, is not to be clearly inferred until we come to the record of the Fourth Day. On the second day (vv. 6-8), the atmosphere was reconstructed. With these lights in existence and with a clear atmosphere, we should infer that they were not yet in a position favorable for giving light to the earth. The atmosphere must have been clarified on the second day and rendered transparent in order to admit the light of the heavenly bodies, yet nothing is said about this. From what is stated about them on the Fourth Day, it seems clear that they did not shine on the earth until this day. They must have been too far away.

On the Fourth Day God commanded lights to function upon the <u>earth</u>. His reason for doing so is stated in verse 14 and 15,

87

which implies that the light, apparently God's eternal light, called forth on the first day, had not performed the functions mentioned in these verses. Evidently this light, being eternal, was not designed to function regularly in a finite world. According to the Scriptures, eternal light shines only temporarily except in the new heaven and the new earth. (Exo. 34:29f; Acts 9:3f; Rev. 21:23.) Eternal light goes with eternal righteousness. In the world called into being during reconstruction week, the time had not yet come for eternal righteousness. Man was to be tested, found wanting, and then created anew as a different creature. Not until all this is accomplished will eternal righteousness with its eternal light appear permanently. Reconstruction week was begun with eternal light; but God who knew the end from the beginning knew that sin would enter the world which He was making at this time. Hence, on the Fourth Day, He made natural light to take the place of eternal light and to serve until all sin shall be done away with.

This natural light was not created at this time. There is no record of creation here; it is stated that the lights were <u>made</u>. They were created in the beginning, as recorded in the statement, "In the beginning God created the heavens and the earth." The stars were created to give natural light. Their light, therefore, would function according to natural law as to rate of transmission, instead of instantaneously. Instantaneous transmission is a characteristic of eternal light only. Only about two per cent of the fixed stars are near enough to the earth for their light to reach the earth in six thousand years, which is the approximate age of the earth since reconstruction week. Many of the stars are so far away that, as we estimate time by our limited methods, we have to state that their light, practically speaking, would never reach the earth. This, then, gives us some idea of the age of the stars and consequently of the age of the creation in the beginning. This should be sufficient evidence to convince any one that the stars could not possibly have been created on the Fourth Day of reconstruction week. This is no reason for supposing that the remainder of the heavenly bodies were not created at the same time that the stars were created (Gen. 1:1).

The reason for making the lights on the Fourth Day is stated in the following words, "And God said, Let there he lights in the firmament of the heaven to divide the day from the night; and let them be for signs, and for seasons, and for days, and for years: And let them be for lights in the firmament of the heaven to give light upon the earth: and it was so."

Let us consider in some detail the reasons here stated for calling these lights into being. They were commanded into being as is shown by the word let. This shows that when the command was given they were already shining but not as God desired they should. Since they were functioning in a way not in accord with His will, their condition was due to sin.

The lights were commanded to give light in the firmament of heaven, or atmosphere. Light was needed on the surface of the earth to serve plant, animal, and human life. This was to continue as long as the finite world should last.

These lights were also to divide the day from the night. This is usually thought of as a completely natural function. We think of the world, as we know it, as being completely adjusted to the condition of alternating day and night. Life, as we observe it, is all adjusted to this, and as we think of it, permanently so. We forget that this condition, permanent as it seems to us, is really but a passing thing. Jesus Himself said that heaven and earth would pass away (Mk. 13:31). With it must pass also all of the finite things dependent upon it such as the forms of life that we know, including man as a finite and sinful being.

Darkness and night are the type of evil and sin. Light and day are the type of law and righteousness. These two types are mutually opposed to each other. They cannot become mingled because they have nothing in common. Hence, the day was divided from the night. The lights might have been distributed in space in such a way as to give a continuous and uniform light upon the earth. Or the night might have been so illumined as to be hardly distinguished from the day. This was not in God's

89

plan. Day and night were to be clearly separated. In the new heaven and the new earth, however, after all sin is done away with, there will be perpetual day in the light of God and of the Lamb. "There shall be no night there." (Rev. 21:25.)

The lights were also to be for seasons, and for days, and for years; three separate periods of time. The lights are spoken of collectively. We have the solar (sun) day and year, also the sidereal (stars, constellations) year and day. There is also the lunar (moon) day and year, periods which are not often mentioned. The Bible does not state which of the three standards we are to use. We use almost entirely a modified form of solar time, which we call mean (middle position) solar time. This custom is based wholly on convenience in civilization.

According to the Scriptures, the lights were to be the measure of the designated periods of time; it is not the light as such, however, which serves this purpose, but the apparent motion of the light-giving bodies concerned. The light they give off enables us to observe their motion and thus to use it for the measurement of time. All time must necessarily be measured by motion.

The lights were to be for seasons. Reading this subjectively, we naturally conclude that the seasons here mentioned are the same as the seasons of the present. This, however, does not follow at all. The seasons of the present time are not perfectly suited to life. They are very important, to be sure, but they could not have been the seasons meant here on the Fourth Day. That the seasons of the Fourth Day were changes is obvious. Of course they were divisions of time just as they are still; but they could not have been climatically the same as the seasons of the present, because this would not have been in harmony with God's other works. Whatever the seasonal changes of climate that existed then, they must have been confined in their variations to the limits of perfect growth of plant and animal life. Also confined to the limits of man's comfort. This variation could not have been very great.

The seasons mentioned on the Fourth Day (v. 14) were due to the inclination of the axis of the earth to the plane of the ecliptic[17], just as it is at present. The axis was set in its present position on this day, and it has remained so ever since.

Towards the close of the seventeenth century, the astronomer Halley advanced a speculation that at the time of the Flood the axis was shifted from a position perpendicular to the plane of the ecliptic to that of an inclination of 23 ½ degrees, which is the position at present. He assumed, without evidence, that a perpendicular position would account for the mild climate previous to the Flood. He also assumed, without evidence, that the shifting of the axis caused the Flood and also changed the climate to that of extremes of heat and cold, as at present.

This speculation has no support whatsoever in science and is no longer even seriously considered. The change from a worldwide mild climate to one of the present extremes is not explained by a shifting of the axis, nor is the rainfall at the time of the Flood thus explained. The principles of meteorology that have been worked out since Halley's time clearly verify this conclusion. The rainfall at the time of the Flood and the change in the climate are explained by a change in atmospheric conditions, not by a change in the position of the earth's axis.

Furthermore, the calculations made by a British astronomer, John B. Dimbleby, at the close of the nineteenth century, show conclusively that the axis has maintained its course in its present position constantly since the Fourth Day. He emphasizes this because it is fully supported by most striking scientific evidence.[18]

First of all, it is stated that the lights were to be "for signs." This part of their purpose, though mentioned first, is usually least

---

[17] The great circle of the celestial sphere that is the path of the sun among the stars of earth as seen from the sun.

[18] John B. Dimbleby, <u>Date</u> <u>of</u> <u>Creation</u> (London: Nister, 1902), pp. 21-23, 69.

considered, if , indeed, it is ever mentioned at all in everyday life. It is natural to neglect the things we do not understand and to believe that because we do not understand them they are of no importance. In secular matters this attitude is often justified. Not so, however, with the Bible. Everything in the record is of importance, whether we understand it or not.

The sun is the type of Jesus in the fullness of His power as it will be when He rules the world. This is indicated in Malachi 4:2 and John 5:35. The moon is the type of the church during the age of grace. The church shines during the night of darkness, which is due to the absence of the Son, though not by its own light; it shines only by the reflected light from the absent Son. The stars typify the lesser light of the individual believers. This light, though feeble, helps to dispel in part the darkness due to the absent Son. The light of His absence is spoken of as the day star (II Peter 1:19). The faith of individual believers during the absence of the Son is referred to as a star in Revelation 2:28.

That the stars speak a language to us is very clearly indicated in the nineteenth Psalm, "Day unto day uttereth speech, and night unto night showeth knowledge. There is no speech nor language where their voice is not heard. Their line is gone out through all the earth, and their words to the end of the world." These highly significant words have been greatly neglected, largely because we have not been able to understand the language of the heavenly bodies. Left to our own lack of wisdom, we should never be able to understand their language. It is not revealed to us in the Bible.

It might be that God did reveal the language of the stars directly to man during the early history of the human race before the Flood. It appears that God named the stars and the constellations. These names have been retained ever since, though thoroughly paganized many centuries ago.

As a result, we think of the origin of names of the stars and constellations as pagan. The pagans did not originate the names; they merely appropriated the names that God had given them long before; but in doing so, they left God's name out and instead invented gods of their own.

It appears that the entire plan of salvation is written in the language of the constellations. Their language portrays the entire history of the human race from its beginning to its full and final redemption. From this we know that the language of the constellations and of the stars is from God.[19]

This, then, is the meaning of the command to let the lights in the firmament of the heaven be for signs. They tell us the full plan of redemption. It was written there in the heavens even before man committed his first sin. We are even justified in concluding that it was written there before the first angel sinned. (Rev. 13:8.) How marvelous are the infinite wisdom and omniscience of God.

Contrast with this the view of the world today regarding the heavenly bodies. It regards them as mainly laboratory material for secular study and investigation. While astronomy continues the study of the heavens with much diligence, as far as the physical aspect is concerned, it does nothing at all to inquire into the meaning of the spiritual side of this great subject. Thus the true meaning of astronomy is lost sight of, and no lasting progress is made because the enlightenment sought is worldly and not from God.

Clarence H. Benson, in his two volumes, The Earth, the Theater of the Universe; and Immensity, lays the foundation in an admirable way for astronomy that is scientific and also Biblical.

"And God made two great lights; the greater light to rule the day, and the lesser light to rule the night; He made the stars also" (v. 16). These lights were not created at this time. They were made in order to rule the day and the night. God made the greater light to rule the day. It is still true that during the day the

---

[19] See The Gospel in the Stars, Joseph A. Seiss (Philadelphia: The Castle Press, 1884).

light of the sun obscures all the other heavenly lights, though at night this is not so fully true of the moon. The rule of the greater light over the day is typical of the Son's rule of the earth. He will rule supreme. All other rule will be set aside.

The rule of the lesser light over the night is typical of the rule of the church during the absence of the Son in the Age of Grace through which we are now passing. It is indeed a lesser light. In the presence of the greater light it would not be seen; but in the absence of the greater light it obscures, either wholly or in part, all other lights. Its light is not its own, but reflected light. During the process most of the light of the church is lost because it is such an imperfect reflector due to sin.

The stars were not made to rule over anything. They are completely subordinate to the greater light, and partly so to the lesser light. This signifies that when the Son rules, individual believers will be wholly subordinate to Him; and while the church rules in the absence of the Son, individual believers are subordinate to it either wholly or in part.

"And God set them in the firmament of the heaven to give light upon the earth, and to rule over the day and over the night, and to divide the light from the darkness" (vv. 17, 18). What do these words signify? Clearly, that the sun, moon, and stars were so placed that they would function as stated.

What does it mean for God to set the sun, moon, and stars? The most obvious meaning is that they were placed in a different position from the one they previously occupied—in order to serve the world that was being reconstructed. The old position, we assume, was not according to Gods's will. It must have been due to sin.

Early in the twentieth century, Dimbleby published a remarkable confirmation of the Scriptures in this respect.[20] This man was an astronomer of great achievement who lived in Wanstead, England and was in close touch with the Greenwich

---

[20] Dimbleby, All Past Time.

Observatory. He made an extended study of the various cycles of astronomical time. Among these were the cycles of time based on the motions of the earth, the moon, and planets, especially those nearest the sun. This led to a study of the eclipse cycles of the sun and the moon, and also of the transits of Mercury and Venus. He calculated the eclipses and the transits to predict their future and past occurrences, just as is ordinarily done by astronomers.

To his surprise, he found that all of these various cycles of time began together: solar time, lunar time, sidereal time, the transits of Mercury and Venus, the precession of the equinoxes, and the period of revolution of the various planets around the sun. There were at least ten different cycles of time, as measured by the motion of the heavenly bodies concerned, which all began together. From this he made the discovery that all of the planets began their present courses of motion around the sun by starting from the same position relative to the sun. In other words, they all began their present motion in their respective orbits by starting in a straight line with reference to each other and the sun and were all in the same relative position.[21]

He found from further calculation that these heavenly bodies would not again come to the same relative position in the future, even in an inconceivably long period of time. Hence, he concluded that the same thing should have been true in the past, unless they had been set or placed in that position. (Job 38:31-33.)

The science of astronomy helps to confirm the remarkable accuracy of the Bible dates commonly referred to as the Ussher dates (verifying the literal interpretation of "days" in Genesis 1).

Finally, when God had finished His work of the Fourth Day, the record says: "And God saw that it was good." The reason for the statement here is similar to that given for the same expression on the first and third days. The reconstructed

---

[21] Siever, p. 6, Figure 1-2.

95

heavenly bodies were good in contrast with their former condition, which was evil because it was due to sin. Calling their reconstructed condition <u>good</u> is equivalent to calling their previous condition <u>evil</u>. As the reconstructed condition was perfectly suited to their future function in the world; namely, the support of life, it was good in this sense also, because in their former condition they could not serve at all.

It is sometimes stated that we cannot know the length of the days of reconstruction week because the word <u>day</u> is sometimes used figuratively to mean much longer periods of time than the literal day. The fact, however, is that such figurative use of the word is always confined to historic time, the time since the creation of man. To speak of prehistoric time when coal was formed, for instance, as the "Day of Coal Plants" would be a usage wholly without precedent. The time under consideration in the account of the Fourth Day is prehistoric; it cannot, therefore, have a figurative application.

The idea of the day as a unit of time is first used in the account of the first day, or period of time; it is divided into two parts, evening and morning. Since this was the customary usage among the Israelites for the literal solar day, we must conclude that this is the meaning intended here. If it meant something else it would be stated otherwise. Even though the sun was not shining on the earth on the first three days, there can be no real reason for not regarding the period as one of equal length with the literal solar day. These three days are spoken of in the same way as the days which follow. Dimbleby's calculations, having proved that these days must be literal, plus the setting of the heavenly bodies in place by God, led to his conclusion that the beginning of all past astronomical time began on the first day of reconstruction week.[22] All scholars are agreed that the word <u>day</u>, as used in verses 14, 16, and 18, is literal.

---

[22] Dimbleby, <u>Date of Creation</u>, pp. 38-53, 88.

96

The literal solar day is due to a definite act of God as recorded. This is the beginning of the system of solar time which man has used ever since; and no one has ever found a substitute for it in the affairs of everyday life. To claim that the Fourth Day is figurative is to violate the plainest rule of usage of language, as well as the simplest rule of reason. If a figure of speech can be introduced here legitimately, then, also, it could be introduced in the Bible elsewhere. In that case we should never agree regarding the real meaning of the Scriptures anywhere.

IX

THE FIFTH DAY
(Genesis 1:20-23)

"And God said, Let the waters bring forth abundantly the moving creature that hath life, and let birds fly above the earth in the open firmament of heaven." (Gen. 1:20 NASV.) This command to the waters to bring forth aquatic animal life is a plain implication that the waters had not been doing this and also that their failure to do so was not in accordance with the will of God; otherwise there should have been no occasion for the command. The waters were commanded to bring forth life abundantly, or to swarm with swarms of living creatures, "Let the waters swarm with swarmers having a living (hayyah-singular) soul (nephesh -that which breathes)."[23]

The animals brought into being on the Fifth Day were all pure and undefiled, because they all came directly by the command of God. It is impossible that God should have created any defiled or unclean animal at any time because it would dishonor Him. Unclean animals are first mentioned in the record of the Flood (Gen. 6:12, 7:2). This was more than sixteen centuries after the sin which caused the corruption of animals entered the world.

"And God created great whales, the great sea monsters and every soul of the living creatures, the creeping ones with which the waters swarm according to their kind, and all the winged birds according to their kind:[24] and God saw that it was good" (v. 21). The word "created" refers to the soul-life ("nephesh

---

[23] Original Hebrew. Animals do not have eternal life.

[24] J. Wash Watts, A Distinctive Translation of Genesis (Grand Rapids: Eerdmans Publ. Co., 1970), p. 18.

hayyah") of animals being brought into existence out of nothing. This verse is God's execution of His own command given in the preceding verse. How simply expressed! How few words to express so great a work! Its very simplicity is what confuses the unbeliever. He is accustomed to thinking in terms of painstaking details. The absence of the details concerning the bringing forth of the animals is to him unthinkable, and, of course, he says he cannot understand it. Nobody understands it. It is a miracle.

Miracles never appeal to unbelievers. This is partly because miracles afford no opportunity, through speculation, for the gratifying of their intellectual pride. Because miracles put the unbeliever to confusion, he will have none of them. Since he feels the need of accounting for the origin of the animals, however, he begins to speculate. He soon seeks to dignify his speculation by expressing it in academic and scientific terms. And, behold, the world has evolution. Evolution violates man's conscience, his senses, and his reason. It is a counterfeit creation. The discussion of it is in Chapter XVI.

Verse 21 states that God created "every living creature that moveth." Surely, these words of the authoritative Book mean just what they say. It seems superfluous to state that a "creature" was <u>created</u>; for creation is clearly implied in the word <u>creature</u>. Why is it stated?

Clearly, it is there for emphasis. Animals could not have come into existence in any other way. If we try to strengthen the Bible by adding man's ideas we weaken it instead. Jesus always quoted the Scriptures just as written, and usually without comment.

It is stated here also that the animals were created according to or <u>after</u> <u>their</u> <u>kind</u>. In a world of order brought into being by the God of perfect law and order, it is understood that animals would all reproduce after their kind. Hence, such a statement need not be made here, and, in fact, it is not made. This passage is often misread, even by believers, who use it in trying to combat evolution. They quote it as saying that the animals were created to reproduce after their kind, and thus they seek to

99

overthrow evolution. It is special creation, however, not a misread account of it that defeats evolution at every point. The actual statement of Genesis is that the animals were <u>created</u> after their kind. That they were to multiply after their kind is understood rather than literally expressed, as explained above.

Since the text does not state that the animals were to <u>multiply</u> after their kind, then what is the purpose of the statement that is made? Since they were created after their kind, the waters would obviously bring them forth in agreement with this. Since this part is too evident to require comment, let us confine our comment to the <u>creation of the animals after their kind</u>.

The statement here discussed is simple when read objectively or wholly on its own merit. There is but one conclusion to draw. They were created according to their previously existing kind or species. If, in their creation, their kind came into existence for the very first time in the world, the expression, <u>after their kind</u>, could not be used. It would simply state that they were created.

The word create is used in only two other places in the first chapter of Genesis. The first of these is in verse 1, which states that in the beginning God <u>created</u> the heavens and the earth. It is <u>not</u> stated that the heavens and the earth were created after their kind. There had never been a former heaven and earth to serve as a pattern. Since the heaven and the earth mentioned here were the first heaven and the first earth (so designated in Revelation 21:1), the simple statement is that they were created. The second place where the word <u>created</u> is used is found in verse 27, where it speaks of the creation of man. Here, also, there is no statement that man was created after his kind. The reason is obvious. There had never been a man before to serve as a kind or pattern for the creation of Adam. The Scriptures actually designate Adam as the first man. "The first man Adam was made a living soul." (I Cor. 15:45.) The very absence of the expression, after his kind, should be considered that Adam was a new order of creation, not a recreation of a former being.

100

Likewise that the creation of the heavens and the earth (Gen. 1:1) was a primal creation.

The account of the creation of animals on the Fifth Day is commonly misunderstood to be an account of the first creation of animals. The Bible nowhere states that these were the first animals; it does state that the heavens and the earth of verse 1 were the first, and that Adam was the first man as already shown.

On the other hand, verse 21 implies very plainly that the animals mentioned there were not the first. The language differs from that in the other two instances in the chapter where the word create is used. In this instance only does it state that the thing created was created <u>after</u> <u>its</u> <u>kind</u>. The kind or species, therefore, had to have a previous existence; otherwise the expression would not be accurate.

The evidence justifies the conclusion that animals had been in existence before those mentioned on the Fifth Day. Why were animals created at this time also? Because the first animals were all destroyed in the flood that ended the great cataclysm implied in verse 2. Remember that the word "create" refers to the soul-life, as previously mentioned, not to their bodies. The plants were not destroyed and so did not have to be created again, as already explained. The animals required food. Evidence that there were plants then is given in the discussion of plants on the third day. (See Chapter VII.)

At the conclusion of verse 21, which tells of God's creation of animals, it is stated, "And God saw that it was good." Since this was pronounced good by the Creator, it follows that it was truly good and not something else.

These animals were in perfect harmony with each other and their surroundings. They were at perfect peace with one another, and in no case did one animal live at the expense of the life of another. There were no carnivorous animals. If there had been, the perfect Creator could not have called good the system of things of which they were a part. Nor could He have done so if they had fought and devoured one another as animals do now.

101

Concerning these animals in their environment, it could be said in the divine sense, "And God saw that it was good."

Sometimes it is maintained that the expression concerning the animal creation of the Fifth Day was made because the animals were suited to man's needs of the present time. Examples are then given, such as beasts of burden or fish or other animals used for food. This interpretation is often carried so far as to speak of certain forms of animal life, such as worms, insects, and so forth, as "good" because they are used as food by other animals that are more useful. It has been shown how certain birds of prey, as the kingfisher and the eagle, are adapted to catching their prey. All of this, however, is a perversion of the meaning good as used in Genesis 1:21 and 25.

Beasts of burden are not mentioned here, nor carnivorous animals of any kind. Man did not need beasts of burden before he sinned, nor did animals prey on one another then. The adaptation of carnivorous animals to the work of capturing and devouring their prey came after man's sin. We cannot believe that God ever created a tiger with the disposition to kill, or with teeth adapted for it, or that He ever created a carnivorous bird with talons suited to the capture of helpless victims and a bill adapted to devouring their flesh. All of this came through sin and the perversion of nature. Volumes have been written to show how perfectly carnivorous animals are adapted to their habits of prey; much has been written to show how these animals came to be adapted to doing this. None of the explanations, however, is satisfactory, and it is seldom that two of them agree. The reason for the failure is that the subject is more than a mere academic matter. It is spiritual and must be understood through Biblical standards.

Let us not deceive ourselves into believing that the animals of the Fifth Day were like the animals of today. To make the matter clear, let it be supposed that God created the lion with the need of the sheep for its food. Then, why was the sheep created with the same kind of instinct for preservation of its life that the lion has? This would make the world a confusion at the very time of creation. Such a world could not stand, because this principle would also prevail throughout the rest of God's creation. God would be the originator of confusion. Indeed, it would make God the creator of the destruction and confusion of every kind that has been in the world since sin entered. Such a thing would lead ultimately to the denial of sin altogether. This very thing is being done today under the guise of philosophy and science.

"And God blessed them, saying, Be fruitful, and multiply, and fill the waters in the seas, and let fowl multiply in the earth" (v.22). The pronouncement, "And God saw that it was good", was not made with the statement of His blessing. There had never been any other kind of blessing in the world to afford a comparison. God's blessings are always perfect.

A blessing always implies contentment and joy. Many of the animals of today are still capable of exercising this feeling. The entrance of sin into the world has not entirely obliterated it. The song of the birds is an example. The joy of a bird in its song seems to be similar to that of a human being. They came from the same Creator.

A blessing was not pronounced upon the plants, for they are not capable of feeling. That pronounced upon the animals was given in connection with their multiplying and filling the earth. It is still seen today to a degree in the mating of birds, the building of their nests, and the rearing of their young, most of which is attended with a condition of peace and satisfaction plainly expressed. What must it have been in the beginning before the first sin!

The blessing included the command to fill the waters and to multiply in the earth. Even under the very adverse conditions of today, animal life has spread to the remotest parts of the land and the sea. There is at least some animal life almost everywhere. This being true at the present time under a climate for the most part hostile, we can only surmise what it was in the beginning, before sin, or even in the early history of the earth before sin had developed to its present extent.

103

No unclean animals are mentioned in the account of animals as given for the fifth day or for the sixth day. Unclean animals are first mentioned at the time of the Deluge after much sin had been in the world for many centuries. (Gen. 65, 7, 11, 12; 7:2.)

The command was that the animals "fill the waters in the seas" and that the "fowl multiply in the earth." Thus the command was more complete for the animals of the seas and those of the air than for those of the land. The evident reason was that man was to occupy the land and that he was not to be hindered in this by animals. Since man was not to live in the seas nor in the air, animals could be freer to multiply in these regions.

Some would have us believe that all animals evolved from lower forms and in a similar manner. This so-called "proof" of evolution is all fictitious and does violence to the most basic principles of true science. There may be a general resemblance between the animals, but this is in no sense whatsoever an evidence of evolution. Similarity does not prove that the higher evolved from the lower through natural processes. If similarity is to be accepted as proof of anything as to origin, it is merely that the similar forms were all created by the same Creator.

The question of the number of species of animals in the world today has long been under consideration. It has been discussed from many standpoints other than that of the Bible. There has never been any agreement, except that it is impossible to fix the number definitely. The difficulties involved in the problem are mainly two. First, animals have for a long time been under the influence of a change in environment which has affected them. Second, there is no agreement as to what constitutes a species. As long as we do not know what the environment was in the past, we shall certainly not make progress in understanding adaptation to it. And as long as we do not know what a species is, we shall not be able to determine the number of species.

A changed environment is an effect of sin. If the animals of the present be viewed from this standpoint, progress can be made in understanding the problem of number of species. The adaptation of the animals originally created to live in a mild climate of lower temperature of varying degree of cold is a second aspect of the problem. As a result of these two factors, almost endless varieties have arisen. In the classification of them, the tendency has been to multiply species needlessly. This has been done because it is considered the easiest method of meeting the difficult problem. As long as the naturalist does not take into consideration the cause of the problem, there is no hope of his reaching any satisfactory conclusion.

If the cause of the complexity of the problem of classification were taken into consideration, progress could be made towards simplification. The result would be to reduce the number of species and increase the number of varieties. Although this would greatly simplify classification, it would not enable any one to determine the exact number of species. It cannot be done until the original environment is restored. We can make only an estimate of what the number was; we are certain, however, that it was very much smaller than it is at the present time.

X

THE SIXTH DAY
(Genesis 1:24-31)

"And God said, Let the earth bring forth the living creature after his kind, cattle, and creeping thing, and beast of the earth after his kind: and it was so" (v. 24). Here for the first time in reconstruction, the earth has a part in the bringing forth of animals. The earth was commanded to bring forth the living creature, cattle, creeping thing, and beast of the earth. A similar command had been given to the waters on the previous day. The earth was commanded to bring them forth after their kind.

The significance of the phrase "after their kind" is quite as evident here as it was in verse 21 in showing that animals like these had previously been created. The evidence for this has already been given. (See Chapter IX.)

"And God made the beast of the earth after his kind, and cattle after their kind, and everything that creepeth upon the earth after their kind" (v. 25). Here we read that the animals named were <u>made</u>, while in verse 21 it states that they were <u>created</u>. Is this consistent? Yes, the two statements are consistent, because both are true. Before reconstruction week the animals had all been destroyed. The animal body was <u>made</u> out of the ground (2:19) according to its previous kind of species. The various species here were not created, as was done the first time. They were only made, fashioned after the previous ones. Now animal <u>life</u> (living soul – <u>nephesh hayyah</u>) had to be brought into being—created, or in other words brought into existence out of nothing. (". . . so that things which are seen were not made of things which do appear" Heb. 11:3.) Hence, what at first thought appears to be an inconsistency proves to be remarkable accuracy. A clear distinction is made here between the use of the words <u>created</u> and <u>made</u>, just as is done in other places in the Scriptures. This is in full keeping with the inspiration of the Scriptures.

The language made after their kind is just as strong evidence of pre-existing animals as that used in verse 21 in connection with the creation of animals. It even goes into details here by stating that the beast of the earth, the cattle, and everything that creepeth upon the earth, were all made after their kind.

The reason animals should be mentioned on two different days is not so evident. That they should be mentioned for the first time in the record of the fifth day is easy to understand. It was then for the first time that the reconstructed world was in condition for them to live. Obviously, they should be created next after the work of the preceding four days. Why should they be mentioned also on the Sixth Day?

The most obvious reason that suggests itself is this: since animals were created to be the closest companions to man of any creature except man, they should also be finally brought into existence on the same day that he was. Man was not created until all other things necessary for his welfare were in order.

Also, on the fifth day the command was to the waters. On the sixth day, the earth was commanded to bring forth the land animals. This could be another reason for the use of two days in this second act of creation.

The Creation of Man

"And God said, Let us make man in our image, after our likeness: and let them have dominion over the fish of the sea, and over the fowl of the air, and over the cattle, and over all the earth, and over every creeping thing that creepeth upon the earth" (v. 26).

The command to bring man into being differs from all of God's other commands. The others were all addressed apparently to some of His various creations which were then being reconstructed to serve His purpose. This command, however, is addressed to "us". Just why should this be done?

107

To whom was God speaking? He must have been addressing the other persons of the Trinity, viz., God the Son; God the Holy Spirit. The Trinity have been together through all eternity.

In verse 26 the inspired record reads in part, "And God said, Let us <u>make</u> man in our image, after our likeness"; while in verse 27 we read, "So God <u>created</u> man in His own image, in the image of God created He him; male and female created He them." Man, therefore, was both <u>made</u> and <u>created</u> in God's image: <u>made</u>, i.e. molded, fashioned in His image as to man's body; <u>created</u> in His image as to the spirit.

We read further in Genesis 2, verse 7, where God's act of bringing man into being is amplified: "And the Lord God <u>formed</u> man of the dust of the ground, and breathed into his nostrils the breath of life ('lives', plural—<u>hayyim</u>, original Hebrew)[25]; and man became a living soul (<u>nephesh</u>-that which breathes)." The act of breathing into his nostrils the breath of lives was a <u>creation</u>; for the life breathed came from the Creator Himself. It became man's spirit. The Triune God, therefore, brought into being man, who is a tri-unity, having spirit, soul, and body (I Thess. 5:23). This, too, is evidence that man was brought into being in the image and likeness of God. Man could not, therefore, have come from the animals. (See Heb. 1:3.)

The following are just a few examples of overstatements and errors that were used by some evolutionist scientists in the past, finally proven wrong:[26]

    a. It is now universally acknowledged that Piltdown man was a hoax. It had been in our textbooks for over forty years as "truth" (M. Bowden, <u>Master Books</u> 1977, El Cajon, Calif., pp. 56-246.)

---

[25] Life that goes on and on—eternal life.

[26] More information and examples can be found in Walter T. Brown, Jr.'s, "<u>In the Beginning</u> . . .". (Phoenix, Center for Scientific Creation, 1989.)

b.   The only evidence we had for Nebraska man turned out to be a pig's tooth. (Duane T. Gish, "Multivariate Analysis: Man . . . Apes . . . Australopithecines . . .", <u>Battle</u> <u>for</u> <u>Creation</u> 1976, San Diego, Creation Life Publishers, pp. 298-305.)

c.   Before 1978, the evidence for Ramapithecus was only a handful of teeth and jaw fragments. Now we know that these fragments were put together incorrectly by Louis Leakey in a form resembling part of the human jaw. Actually, Ramapithecus was just an ape (Gish, "Richard Leakey's Skull", <u>Battle</u> <u>for</u> <u>Creation</u> 1976, pp. 193-200); (Allen L. Hammond, "Tales of an Elusive Ancestor", <u>Science</u> <u>83</u> November 1983, pp. 37, 43); (Adrienne L. Zihlman and J. Lowenstein, "False Start of the Human Parade", <u>Natural</u> <u>History</u>, Aug/Sept 1979, pp. 86-91.)

d.   Java "man," discovered by Eugene Dubois, has been acknowledged by him (forty years later) to be probably a large gibbon (tall, thin ape). Debois also admitted that he had withheld parts of four other thigh bones of apes, found in the same area, that supports this conclusion (Eugene Dubois, <u>Man</u>, Vol. 37, January 1937, pp. 4, 5.)

e.   Many experts consider the fossils of Peking man to be the remains of apes which were decapitated and exploited for food by true man (Patrick O'Connell, <u>Science</u> <u>of</u> <u>Today</u> 1969, pp. 108-138.)

f.   "Skull 1470," discovered by Richard Leakey, is more humanlike and yet older than Homo erectus (Java man and Peking Man) and Australopithecines. Evolution does not have man evolving quite that soon (<u>National</u> <u>Geographic</u>, June 1973, p. 819); (William R. Fix, <u>The</u> <u>Bone</u> <u>Peddlers</u> 1984, Macmillan Publishing Company, NY, pp. 50-61.)

g.   The recent discovery of Homo habilis shows this animal to be clearly apelike in proportions and should never have been classified as Homo [man] (Donald C. Johnson et al., <u>Nature</u>, Vol. 327, 21 May 1987, pp. 205-209.)

h. Detailed computer studies have shown that the Australopithecines are not intermediate between man and living apes. The study of an entire anatomy, not just knee joints, shows that they probably swung from the trees. The Australopithecines, made famous by Louis and Mary Leakey, are a type of extinct ape (Solly Zuckerman, Evolution as a Process 1954, George Allen and Unwin Ltd., London, p. 307.)

i. For 100 years we were led to believe that Neanderthal man was stooped and apelike. Recent studies show that some Neanderthal men were crippled with arthritis and rickets. Neanderthal, Heidelberg, and Cro-Magnon men were completely human. Artists' depictions of them and techniques used to date these fossils are highly questionable (Francis Ivanhoe, "Was Virchow Right About Neanderthal?", Nature, Vol. 227, 8 August 1970, pp. 577, 578; William L. Straus, Jr. and A.J.E. Cave, Pathology and the Posture of Neanderthal Man", The Quarterly Review of Biology, December 1957, pp. 348-363; Boyce Rensberger, "Facing the Past", Science 81, October 1981, p. 49.)

The account of the creation of man starts with a command beginning with let, thus implying that there was hindrance to God's will. What is the reason for it? We can understand why the previous commands implied hindrance to His will; for in every case He was overcoming the consequences of sin. Here, He was creating the first man who, of course, should be perfect. What in this case was the hindrance due to sin?

Although God was creating the first man, He was not creating him as the first ruler of the earth. The first being created to rule the earth was Lucifer. Because of the first ruler's sin, God was now creating another to take his place. Plainly, it was Lucifer's sin, therefore, that was the hindrance to the Creator at this time.

Man was created to be the ruler over all of the animals and also over all the earth. This is plainly stated. Man is still naturally a ruler. He is usually eager to assume authority over something. He likes to be elected or appointed to office. He wants to be an officer of some kind so he can rule. This trait is even observed in children at their games.

Just how man was to have dominion over all the animals is not stated, though it may easily be inferred. At the time under consideration the animals were all at perfect peace with each other and with man. Hence, man through his greater intelligence and his greater love would soon know how to win the animals and thus cause them willingly to do his bidding. Animals were created to respond to love, and they soon learn where to find it. Man was not to rule them by fear as he does so frequently in the present age.

"And God blessed them, and God said unto them, Be fruitful, and multiply, and replenish the earth, and subdue it: and have dominion over the fish of the sea, and over the fowl of the air, and over every living thing that moveth upon the earth" (v. 28). This shows that man's dominion over the animals is right, because God commanded it. Of course, it was the command to a sinless man to rule over innocent animals.

As soon as man was created, God blessed him, both male and female. A blessing pronounced by God certainly can mean nothing short of a promise of the greatest of joy. God had pronounced a blessing upon animals in connection with their fruitfulness and their multiplying. Now He pronounces a similar blessing on man. Man is capable of far greater joy than the animals. The Holy Spirit can dwell in him, and the fruit of the Spirit is joy. Innocent man is capable of far more joy than sinful man.

How great man's joy was after he received the blessing of God can be imagined only in part. We are now too sinful to comprehend it; only when we become like Him shall we fully understand. We can, however, at least appreciate the fact that before sin entered man's heart he was perfectly happy and

111

innocent in carrying out God's command to multiply. It was sin alone that brought about the present condition of suffering and shame.

The question is often asked, What is meant by "replenish the earth"? Some have claimed that this means that there had been a pre-Adamic race of people on the earth, who were all destroyed; hence, there came this command to replenish the earth with people. This, however, is not true, else it would have been revealed to us.

The primary meaning of the word in the original, that is here translated <u>replenish</u>, is to <u>fill</u>. It is, however, also translated <u>replenish</u> when the context so requires. The very same word in the original was used in God's command to Noah after the Flood. Noah was commanded to be fruitful, and multiply, and <u>replenish</u> the earth (Gen. 9:1). In this latter case, then, the context requires the rendering <u>replenish</u> because the world had been destroyed by the Flood; and so the command meant that the earth was to be filled again—<u>replenished</u>.

In considering the command to Adam, we are mindful that he was the first man; but he was not the first ruler of the earth. The first ruler was Lucifer, and with him there were hosts of angels. They fell, through sin, and lost their right to have dominion over the earth. The earth was now to be <u>filled</u> (NASV).

"And God said, Behold, I have given you every herb bearing seed, which is upon the face of all the earth, and every tree, in the which is the fruit of a tree yielding seed; to you it shall be for meat (food" (v. 29). This shows clearly that man was created to eat both herb and the fruit of every tree in all the earth. No exceptions were made. We have no right to add to the record. Hence we know that there were no poisonous plants as there are now. Nor were they any nonedible seeds and fruits. It states that the seed of <u>every</u> <u>herb</u> and the fruit of <u>every</u> <u>tree</u> were given to man for his meat or food. This was just as should be expected in a perfect world. It is easy to understand when read objectively,

112

though confusing if read in the light of subjective experience gained in our world of sin (Isa. 55:8, 9).

The food, called meat, was given to man. Man was not left to find it and take it as is usually his custom now. It is stated plainly that God gave man his food in the beginning. It is still customary for people of Christian culture to regard their food as a gift from God, and they thank Him for it.

God's wisdom is shown in His creating seeds to serve the double purpose of reproducing the plant and of supplying man with his food. The substance of the seed is food for the young seedling before it is able to make its own food. And yet this same substance is food for man for his growth and to enable him to live. The substance is made from water, carbon dioxide, sometimes nitrogen and other elements, also mineral matter from the ground. The plant takes these substances from the air and the ground and makes them into food for itself and for man. It produces enough seed for both purposes.

The fruit serves but a small purpose in the economy of the plant. In the production of such fruits as the apple, pear, and peach, or the pumpkin and the melon, much energy has been spent that is of no use to the plant. The seeds might have been encased far more economically as far as the need of the plant is concerned. The banana is a still more striking example; here the seeds are not fertile and, hence, are of no use to the plant. They do not need to be encased and protected. Yet they are encased with a substance in great abundance that serves for man's food, just as is the case with the apple, pear, orange, melon, and other fruits. The plant makes what it needs and more. It makes for man the food that he cannot make for himself.

The world, as God created it, was a unified world. It would still be such if sin had not entered it. Our present world, which is a world of sin, is not fully unified. Many plants, such as those of the parasitic class, live at the expense of other plants. Man lives at the expense of some of the animals, and many of the animals live by destroying other animals. Many of the physical forces in the world of today are mutually opposed to each other. One

113

destroys what another builds up. This was not the case when man was created.

"And to every beast of the earth, and to every foul of the air, and to every thing that creepeth upon the earth, wherein there is life, I have given every green herb for meat: and it was so" (v. 30). This is God's provision for food for the animals. In the record we see that provision is made for every beast of the earth, no matter where it lives, and for the fowl of the air and every thing that creeps upon the earth. The food given to them was the green herb. The Bible does not mention any part of the green herb; hence it must mean just what it states and that is the entire plant. This includes the seed and grain. The significant thing to notice is that no exception is made among the class of plants given. It was every green herb that was to serve for the food of animals. The animals did not have to avoid poisonous plants as they do now. For example, animals today must avoid eating Jimson weed, skunk cabbage, nightshade, tobacco, and many other plants. They have been endowed with a sense of self-protection which we call instinct.

The world of the time before sin was so different from that of the present that we cannot adequately imagine it even with respect to the animals. For this reason we find it so difficult to conceive what it will be in this respect during the Millennium. That will be a time when sin will not rule the world. Instead, the world will be under the rule of righteousness. Much of the sin will be done away with; also the consequences of sin. The years of childhood will be lengthened (Isa. 65:20). Sin will be a reproach. Now it is often held as a virtue.

Health will be a common thing because of righteousness. "Then shall thy light break forth as the morning, and thine health shall spring forth speedily." (Isa. 58:8.) "Instead of the thorn shall come up the fir tree, and instead of the brier shall come up the myrtle tree: and it shall be to the Lord for a name, for an everlasting sign that shall not be cut off." (Isa. 55:13.) "Behold, I will do a new thing . . . I will even make a way in the wilderness, and rivers in the desert." (Isa. 43:19.) "The wolf also shall dwell with the lamb , and the leopard shall lie down with the kid; and the calf and the young lion and the fatling together; and a little child shall lead them.

"And the cow and the bear shall feed; their young ones shall lie down together: and the lion shall eat straw like an ox . . . : for the earth shall be full of the knowledge of the Lord, as the waters cover the sea." (Isa. 11:6-9.)

There will be no carnivorous animals. "They shall not hurt nor destroy in all My holy mountain: . . ." (Isa. 11:9). Animals that are now at enmity with each other and with man will be at peace.

The record of the events of the Sixth Day closes thus: "And God saw everything that He had made, and, behold, it was very good." (Gen. 1:31a.)

This final pronouncement of very good, it must be noted, was the last of God's recorded acts at the close of His six days of work. This pronouncement was a general one, whereas the previous ones were specific. Furthermore, it was pronounced only on what God had made; not on what He had created. That was more than very good; it was perfect. It would be superfluous in the record to mention its perfection, for it was pure and undefiled right before the beginning.

XI

THE SEVENTH DAY
(Genesis 2:2, 3)

"Thus the heavens and the earth were finished, and all the host of them." (Gen. 2:1.)

It is in the nature of things, even in the world of the present time, to experience satisfaction upon the completion of a task undertaken. In a human way we experience this also as we contemplate the meaning of the words just quoted.

"And on the Seventh Day God ended His work which He had made. And God blessed the seventh day, and sanctified it" (v.3). These words tell us that God pronounced a blessing on the Seventh Day. He did not bless the six days, however, nor sanctify them. If no sin had ever entered the world before this time, we believe there would have been no reason for distinguishing between the seven days as God does. He makes a very clear distinction and at the same time gives His reason for it, which is, "because that in it (the Seventh Day) He had rested from all His work which God created and made" (v.3).

The only things God <u>had</u> <u>created</u> during the six days were blessed at the time of their creation. These were the animals and man. The things He <u>had</u> <u>made</u> were not so blessed. And now at the close of the six days He did not bless these days as a whole, nor does He bless them in any other way. Neither did He bless the new system of things instituted nor any of His works that He <u>had</u> <u>made</u>. He merely blessed the Seventh Day after it was past, but did not include the other six days which were also past. The fact that the Seventh Day was already past when the blessing upon it was pronounced is shown by the tense, <u>had</u> <u>rested</u>, used in stating the reason for the blessing. The Seventh Day is first mentioned in verse 2. Verse 3 refers to a time later than the Seventh Day.

Evidently the Seventh Day was a satisfaction to God in a very different manner from that of the six days. The six days were not a joy at all, because they carried with them the problem of sin.

The work which God accomplished during the six days was done by stages—a succession of acts. The work as a whole was a process. However, the two acts of creation on the fifth and sixth days were, in the nature of the case, instantaneous.

An act of finite creation can never be a succession of events. Nor can it be a process. It is a miracle. Miracles are instantaneous and thus preclude all possibility of being a succession of events or of being a process of any kind. Miracles consume no time. Successive events and processes do consume time. From the record given us we know that God's work of the six days was not identical with His act of original creation in the beginning, which is recorded in Genesis 1:1. If His work of the six days was primal creation, everything done would have been included in a single instantaneous act. Otherwise, He would have limited Himself to time without a reason.

The heavens and the earth were <u>created</u> in the beginning (Gen. 1:1). They were <u>made</u> or <u>reconstructed</u> on the first, second, third, and fourth days. And they were <u>finished</u> on the sixth day when man was created to rule the earth. The word <u>finish</u> implies a process of work through stages. The word <u>create</u> does not occur anywhere in the account of the heaven and the earth as given in the record of the first four days. Nor does it occur in any other Scriptures which refer to the work of these four days. In reference to the heavens and the earth on the four days the word used is <u>made</u>. And this requires pre-existing material with which to work. Such material, no matter what its condition, could not have been in a condition that was in accord with God's will, otherwise He would not have refashioned it. Disorder is always due to sin. Sin is a source of grief to God. As evidence of this, read the reason given for the destruction of the world through the Flood. (Gen. 6:5-7), especially verse 6.) The consequences of sin are also a grief to Him. When He deals

117

with sin or with its consequences, His grief is shown in His Word.

God's grief over sin and the results of sin is one of the things that we most overlook. Sometimes even the converted do not think of Him as they should. The unconverted never give any serious thought to the grief God suffers because of their course. This spirit prevails often in children when they do not think of the sorrow their wrong conduct causes their parents. In the same manner, grown people have to be taught to regard the grief to God which results from their sin.

We can know God's feelings by observing His deeds and His words just as we know the feelings of our fellow man. Let us not suppose that this need not be taken into account in the record of Genesis before the sin of man. God is always the same as to the nature of His deeds and words. A study of this should be made by those who would understand the problem of sin.

When God creates, it is a joy both to Himself as the Creator and also to the creature. This must be true because it is all in keeping with the divine plan of things. The creature is not fashioned out of some other creature that has passed through sin. No, the creature is brought into being when nothing of its kind exists. It is brought into existence wholly new and perfect— hence the joy over it.

When God created the animals, He pronounced a blessing upon them at once. To pronounce a blessing upon someone or something is joy to Him, indeed even to us. When God created man, He again pronounced His blessing upon His new creature. This too was a joy. Doubtless it was a greater joy than that at the creation of the animals, because man was a greater being. When God created the earth as referred to in the words, "When I laid the foundations of the earth" (Job 38:4), this being the time mentioned in Genesis 1:1 and Hebrews 1:10, it was also an occasion for the greatest joy of all; for the record states that it was the time "when the morning stars sang together, and all the sons of God shouted for joy" (Job 38:7). At the creation of the earth the angels were present. The joy which followed creation in the beginning is far beyond human comprehension. It was divine and angelic joy. No such joy is mentioned at the time of the other recorded acts of creation as found in verses 21 and 27, when the animals and man were created.

When God made or reconstructed anything, no blessing was ever pronounced upon it—none when He made the firmament on the second day; and none when He made the lights on the fourth day. Nor was any blessing pronounced upon anything that was brought into being by ordering it as the light on the first day, the separation of the seas and the dry land, then the plants on the third day. God did not pronounce a blessing upon these as a finished thing at the close of the sixth day, when He observed everything He had made, and said that it was very good. If what God Himself pronounced "very good" after He had finished it was allowed to go without a blessing pronounced upon it, there surely must have been a good reason. God has a good reason for all that He does. The reason we suggest in this case was that He knew He was dealing with the result of sin, and it grieved Him.

He knew also that the whole system would still have to be tested and would be found wanting. He knew that, finally, it would all have to pass away and that He would have to create all things new. The six days were the type of the period of sin that was to follow, a day for a thousand years (II Peter 3:8). The Seventh Day was the type of the Millennium or seventh thousand years. This will be the time when God and His children will rest from carrying the burden of sin. They will rule fully over sin instead of being under its burden. The Seventh Day was set apart as God's day, because it stands for the things that are fully His own. To distinguish between this day and the other days that were not so set apart, God blessed the Seventh Day and sanctified it. This day stands for sinlessness, but the others are all connected with sin.

This is fully confirmed by other Scriptures as well as by Genesis. "By the word of the Lord were the heavens made; and all the host of them by the breath of His mouth. He gathereth the waters of the sea together as an heap: He layeth up the depth in

119

storehouses. Let all the earth fear the Lord: let all the inhabitants of the world stand in awe of Him. For He spake, and it was done; He commanded, and it stood fast." (Psalm 33:6-9.) This refers to the making of the heavens as begun on the second day and finished on the fourth day. In the record concerning both days the word made occurs. And in both instances it states that God made. The Psalm is in exact agreement with the account in Genesis. The gathering together of the waters unto one place on the third day was done by God's command and was not an act of creation.

We note that these Scriptures are introduced by the words, "He loveth righteousness and judgment" (v. 5). This implies that He is grieved with unrighteousness. He loves judgment but is grieved over the necessity for exercising it. The context is one of dealing with sin. The words "He spake and it was done; He commanded and it stood fast", imply a command. The command is introduced by these significant words, "Let all the earth fear the Lord: let all the inhabitants of the world stand in awe of Him." The fear and the awe of the Lord are necessary only where sin exists. From all this we conclude that When the Lord made the heavens and when He commanded the seas and the dry land into being, sin was already in existence.

"Happy is he that hath the God of Jacob for his help, whose hope is in the Lord his God: Which made heaven, and earth, the sea, and all that therein is: which keepeth truth for ever." (Psa. 146:5, 6.) The context of this Psalm is one of sin. The God of Jacob had to deal with sin constantly. The next verse speaks of God executing judgment for the oppressed. This makes it entirely clear that the context is one of sin. And in the midst of this context verse 6 speaks of the God "which made heaven, and earth, the sea, and all that therein is." Here, again, God's acts of making or reconstruction go with the result of sin. There is no other conclusion to draw.

We observed that when God created the world there was joy, and praise, and song, and blessing (Job 38:4-7). In contrast, when the word was made, or refashioned, no joy, no praise, no

120

song, and no blessing are mentioned anywhere. God was grieved when He reconstructed the world. This is most plainly shown in His deeds and verified by His words, both expressed and unexpressed. Oh, that we might all learn to honor Him by our deeds and to express it by our words, and to refrain from dishonoring Him as we most surely do when we read His Holy Word carelessly after the traditions of men.

Thus it is found even after a brief examination of the Scriptures related that there is abundant evidence to show why the Seventh Day differs from the six days. It was a day on which God ended His work which He had made, and also the day on which He rested from all His work which He had created and made.

There is also abundant reason for the distinction made between the use of the words create and make. The distinction made proves the inspiration of the Scriptures by making everything harmonize. There is thus perfect harmony between the various passages of Genesis. Yet, at the same time, all of these passages harmonize with the passages outside of Genesis, such as the Psalms. Without the distinction, there is confusion instead of harmony and inspiration. We must make our choice between accuracy and inaccuracy. A distinction between the Seventh Day and the six days is essential for this reason.

God's rest is associated with His blessing and with sanctity. He was pleased with it, for He could not pronounce a blessing without being happy Himself at the same time. God's act of primal creation (Gen. 1:1) is never called work either. That act preceded the entrance of sin into the world; and for this reason it had, of course, nothing at all to do with sin.

Yet, when God blessed the Seventh Day, He designated all of His acts of the six days as work; for He speaks of His work which He created and made. The two acts of creation here referred to, the creation of the animals and the creation of man, were not wholly a joy to Him because the animals were created to replace those that had been destroyed; and man was created to take the place of the ruler of the earth who sinned. Hence, these two acts of creation were called work, even though He expressed His pleasure at the time by pronouncing a blessing on each creation, both man and beast. That these two acts of creation differed from the first creation is shown by the fact that at the creation of the animals and of man there was no expression of joy on the part of any other of His creatures. The morning stars did not sing together, nor did the sons of God shout for joy.

A being of infinite and, therefore, inexhaustible power could not feel fatigue or have need of rest such as we do. It was not ordinary rest that God needed. He needed spiritual rest, rest from His grief over sin and its results. He took one day for this purpose after He had worked six days. What He did on the succeeding days is not given under a list of numbered days. That He resumed His work in a world of sin is plain from the words of Jesus, "My Father is working until now, and I Myself am working."[27] (John 5:17 NASV.) God could never cease from work as long as there is sin in the world.

There is abundant evidence in the Scriptures to show that God feels the burden of man's sin. When the woman with the issue of blood for twelve years came behind Jesus and touched the border of His garment and was healed, Jesus felt the effect in His own body; for He at once said, "Somebody hath touched Me: for I perceive that virtue (power) is gone out of Me." (Luke 8:46.) When He learned from her that she was healed, He said to her, "Daughter, be of good comfort: thy faith hath made thee whole; go in peace" (v. 48). He bore her burden of illness. The burden of healing the sick Jesus called work, even when He did it on the Sabbath day.[28]

Here it is very clear that when sickness, which is a result of sin, is healed, Jesus Himself calls it work. He was God and He likened His work to that of the Father. Therefore, we know that when God speaks of His <u>work</u>, He is speaking of overcoming the

---

[27] See also John 9:4.

[28] John 5:5-9, 16, 17.

consequences of sin. This is plainly what is meant by the word work as used in Genesis 2:2, 3, where it refers to all that He did during the six days.

That this work was a burden to God is shown in the fact that after He had rested on the Seventh Day he "was refreshed" (Ex. 31:17). Omnipotent power applied to a finite task needs no rest in order to be refreshed where there is no sin to hinder and grieve. Nor is there any reason for calling the application of the divine power, work, unless there is sin in the way to obstruct. Not even man's activity was called work until after he had sinned. After sin, man's efforts were mainly from necessity instead of from choice, especially such efforts as those involved in making a living. This is work (Ex. 20:9, 10; 23:12 and other passages).

Some theologians hold that the Seventh Day is still continuing and that God is still resting, mainly because the record for the Seventh Day does not close with any statement regarding the evening and the morning. This is done in open disregard of the Bible. There are many objections to the view, but all these are overlooked. Some of the objections are the following:

(1) Inasmuch as God blessed and sanctified the Seventh Day, He was pleased with it. If the Seventh Day is still continuing, then it has God's blessing and sanctification on it. Hence, it would follow that God is pleased with the civilization of the present time as well as with that of all historic time. Thus God's approval would rest on all of its sin, and He would do nothing to remedy it for at least the length of the Seventh Day as an aeon (many millions of years, at least as long as each of the six preceding periods). If God is resting during all of the seventh period, He is indifferent to man's sin during all of this time. To maintain that He is thus indifferent is directly to oppose the Scriptures.

(2) When Jesus was on earth, He predicted His death, resurrection, and return to earth to rule it in righteousness. He commanded everybody, especially His followers, to prepare for

His return and to watch for it. If the Seventh Day is an aeon still continuing, then it has scarcely begun yet, for man has been in existence only about six thousand years. This length of time is scarcely the beginning of an aeon that must run for many millions of years. The purpose of His return is to rule the earth in righteousness. This He would not do while He is still resting. Hence, His return would not take place until the close of the seventh aeon, which would be many millions of years in the future. Such doctrine results in indifference to the Lord's return, even to the ignoring of it entirely. Here, again, the doctrine is directly opposed to the Scriptures. It opposes all that Jesus taught regarding His return.

(3) The assertion that the seven days are aeons is only speculation. It has never been established, nor can it ever be established. There are numerous objections to it. Some of these are taken up in Chapter XII.

(4) In addition to what has just been set forth, the assertion also does violence to the accuracy of the Scriptures. In Genesis 2:2 we read, "And on the seventh day God <u>ended</u> <u>His</u> <u>work</u> which He had made." Then, on the authority of this statement, on the Seventh Day God ended His work of the six days and also rested from it. The two verbs, <u>ended</u> and <u>rested</u>, are in the same tense and treated alike. If His work was ended at the time referred to in the statement, then His rest also was ended and could not be still continuing.

It is stated in verse 3 that God blessed and sanctified the Seventh Day because "in it He <u>had</u> <u>rested</u> from all His work." It follows again that at the time here referred to God <u>had</u> <u>rested</u> from all His work. The verb, <u>had</u> <u>rested</u>, means that His rest was <u>already completed</u>. This precludes all possibility of claiming that God's rest is still continuing. To assert that it is still going on is to disregard completely the statement of the Bible; for the Bible states that at the time when "the heavens and the earth were finished and all the host of them" (Gen. 2:1), God's work was not only ended, but His rest from it also was ended. As soon as sin entered the reconstructed world, God resumed work (John

124

5:17). Every time He heals the sick, it is, in a sense, an act of creation. And every time He saves a lost sinner unto life eternal, it is an act of new creation necessitated by the sin that followed the first seven days. It is, therefore, not true that God ceased from all work of creation at the close of the sixth day. Nor that He has continued His rest ever since that time.

(5) Why is the expression, evening and morning, omitted from the Seventh Day? On each of the six days the record gives the several acts of God and the events for the day. For example, on the first day: Let there be light; God saw the light that it was good; God divided the light from the darkness; God called the light Day and the darkness Night. This is the list of recorded events for the first day. There were each instantaneous, yet the series of events was distributed over the period of one day made up of an evening (night) and a morning (daylight). Hence, to make this fact clear, the record of events for the day is followed by the statement, "And the evening and the morning were (constituted) the first day." Thus the record for the first day is complete and understandable. The six days on which God worked are all treated in the same way. The succession of days was established, and the reconstructed world was then complete. The days, each composed of an evening or night followed by a morning or daylight, were established to succeed each other regularly and indefinitely.

God rested on the Seventh Day, however, and made this fact a part of the record for the week. After His work, rest was necessary. He had to be refreshed (Ex. 31:17) from His grief over the sin which made this work necessary, and thus be restored to His former state.

On the Seventh Day He did not do any work at all. Hence, there were no acts of His nor events to record, and no occasion to state that they were distributed over the evening and the morning for this day. There was no more occasion to mention the fact of the evening and the morning for the Seventh Day than there was to mention any of the other things brought into being during the six days, as for example to state that the seas and the land were still separated, or that the plants and other forms of life were still living. God made the Seventh Day a perfect one, and recorded nothing at all except the fact that He rested, which was evidently the only purpose of the day.

(6) According to the Genesis account, man's sin did not occur until after the Seventh Day. It is not mentioned until after the account for this day. Man's first sin called forth at once God's work of dealing with it. If this had taken place on the Seventh Day, it would have been a most grievous disturbance of His rest and it would be mentioned in the record. We are certain that man's sin did not occur until <u>after</u> <u>the</u> <u>Seventh</u> <u>Day</u>.

If the Seventh Day is still continuing, then we face the absurdity that man's <u>sin has</u> <u>not</u> <u>yet</u> <u>entered</u> <u>the</u> <u>world</u>! To assert that God is still resting is only a speculation. It has never been harmonized with the accuracy and inspiration of the Bible; nor can this ever be done. It must be evident that the assertion is only a disguised attempt to set the inspiration aside.

In concluding this Chapter it should be observed that the new order of things, while perfect, was nevertheless conditional perfection in a finite world that had already been under the influence of sin. The perfection was conditioned on the obedience of the newly created ruler. The world here referred to was not eternal. It was possible for further sin to enter it. The omniscient God knew that sin would enter, and He had the remedy provided in "the Lamb slain from the foundation of the world " (Rev. 13:8).

XII

THE SEVEN DAYS OF GENESIS WERE NOT AGES OR AEONS

The expression "days of creation" is very commonly understood to mean an undefined period of time in which God created all things. More correctly, it is applied to the days mentioned in the first two chapters of Genesis, which are ofttimes called "creation week". The designation "creation week" is not found in the Bible itself. The expression is correct only in the sense that it was the time of the creation of man. Only one other act of creation is recorded in the entire week, that of animals on the fifth day. All of the other acts of that week were direct acts of reconstruction. Even the creation of the animals was in one sense an act of reconstruction, for the first animals had been destroyed. The same is true of the creation of man; for by this creation the former ruler of the earth was replaced by a new ruler, the former through his own sin having lost his right to rule. Since everything done on the seven days was in some way an act of reconstruction, the period is most clearly understood as Reconstruction Week.

It is commonly held that science clearly shows that creation covered a very long and indefinite period. Many think it is necessary to extend the days over a long period of time in order to harmonize Genesis with science. In this manner science and Genesis, usually held to be in opposition, are said to be brought into agreement. The assertion is frequently made also that it is a matter of no serious consequence whether one regards the seven days of Genesis as literal days or not. The question is declared to be wholly a matter of scholarship. Since scholarship is quite generally opposed to the literal interpretation of "days", many have been led to believe that they must necessarily accept the "long period" view lest they expose their ignorance.

Previous to the nineteenth century, the question of days versus long periods was scarcely regarded as a question for discussion, because practically everybody believed the seven days to be literal, based almost entirely upon faith in the Bible. The Word was believed to mean just what it said. It was regarded as a book of authority, and there was no question regarding its literal meaning in anything where the context did not clearly show it to be figurative.

With the advance of secular education and with the discoveries of science in various fields, doubt gradually arose regarding the literal interpretation. We must note that the doubt did not arise out of a sincere effort to understand the Bible better; nor did doubters propose to render a fuller and greater service to God. As this type of education was developed mainly by unbelievers, it was impossible for it to result in anything else. The unbelieving heart cannot establish in others a faith which it does not accept itself. In this, as is everything else, a thing cannot produce that which it does not possess.

As scientific discoveries progressed, especially in geology, there was an increasing accumulation of evidence showing that the history of the earth has extended over a very long time. The evidence is very conclusive that such a period elapsed from the creation of the heavens and the earth in the beginning to the creation of man. Unfortunately, it has usually been assumed by scientists that the Bible states that the world and all it contains was created about six thousand years ago, and that all of it was brought into being in six literal days. This erroneous assumption has caused great harm. It has led many to conclude that science has triumphed over the Bible in discovering the truth pertaining to the history of the earth, so-called "creation evolution."

As long as it was thought impossible by means of evolution to disprove the literal interpretation of the "days" of Genesis, evolution could make no progress before the public. It must be observed here that public sentiment is what evolution is compelled to depend on for its progress and not scientific discoveries; for of the latter it has made none at all. We should note further that the decline of the church has developed most rapidly during the period in which evolution has been so widely accepted.

Usually the so-called "scientific" account of creation is preferred because it is regarded as natural, whereas the Scriptural account is considered miraculous. At first thought, the so-called "natural" seems plausible enough to appeal to many. In order to have a better understanding of this, before going further, let us consider briefly some essentials usually overlooked regarding the natural.

Life defies definition because it is a miracle. The inanimate world of nature proves upon analysis to be founded upon time, space, and energy; three things that science has never been able to account for, nor to trace to their ultimate source, for the source is inseparably bound to the miraculous. A little reflection must convince any one that nature is likewise bound to the miraculous. Hence, any attempt to avoid the miraculous by turning from the Bible to science is only to turn from miracles in one place to find them everywhere else.

The failure of the scientist in interpreting Genesis, and his subsequent rejection of it altogether, has been due partly to erroneous theological views. Unfortunately, in recent years, theologians have often attempted to interpret Genesis in the light of scientific discoveries which they themselves did not understand and therefore could not evaluate correctly. They have tried to reconcile Genesis with scientific discoveries merely on the general acceptance of the latter without being able to consider them on their real merits. In order to do this, it was considered necessary to introduce the idea that the seven days of Genesis represent long periods of time or aeons. This has wrought confusion both in science and in theology. Both true science and true theology are a part of the truth and must be in agreement. There can never be any disagreement between God's creation and His revealed Word.

129

On the assumption that the seven days of Genesis are aeons, or geological ages, let us see what the consequences would be as viewed from the standpoint of geology. In geology it is self-evident that a long period of time, such as an aeon, must leave its characteristic record in the rock formations of that time. Hence, it would necessarily follow that the rock formation would correspond to the Genesis account for each aeon-day involved. Let us consider the seven days in this light:

<u>First</u> <u>Day</u>. There was water over the face of the whole earth during the entire period. Therefore, there were no shore-lines—hence, no shore deposits. The deposits possible under the conditions prevailing were those of the open sea. This would be very little and all of a fine texture. If the speculation assumes that meteorites fell then as they do now, they would be found intermingled with the fine sediment. This formation would be the oldest and, therefore, it would be found at the bottom of all sedimentary formations.

<u>Second</u> <u>Day</u>. During this period the sea continued to cover the whole earth just as it did during the first period. Hence, the rock formation would be the same. It would be an unbroken continuation of that of the first period, with no physical evidence to mark their time separation. Yet the Genesis account makes a clear time distinction between the two periods.

<u>Third</u> <u>Day</u>. During this period dry land appeared above the water for the first time. Hence, this was the time when shore lines were first in evidence and should contain characteristic deposits such as silt, clay, sand, gravel, pebbles, shingle, boulders, and so forth. It would be during this period that fossils should first be found; and they would be fossils of plants only because, according to the speculation, no other form of life yet existed.

<u>Fourth</u> <u>Day</u>. The conditions for rock formation and fossilization would continue unbroken from the Third Period, resulting in an unbroken continuation of the same rock formation. There would be no physical mark of separation between them. Yet the Genesis account would require such

130

separation because, in point of time, they are clearly distinguished here.

Fifth Day. Conditions for rock formation would continue unbroken as begun in the Third Period. Only one distinct change would be found, that of animal fossils in addition to plant fossils. These fossils, however, would not appear until about two-thirds of the period for sedimentary rock formation had passed.

Sixth Day. Every condition prevailing at the close of the Fifth Period would continue during the Sixth. There would be just one additional condition, that of man living towards the close of the Period. The evidence of his activities would be found and designated as fossils. The time including man's existence also would be designated an aeon.

Seventh Day. Conditions as they existed at the close of the Sixth Period would continue through the Seventh, except that this was a period of rest for the Creator as contrasted with the previous Six Periods of work. This would mean that the natural world continued in a uniform and undisturbed condition for this, the final Period. Incidentally, if the day be taken to mean an aeon, and an aeon consists of millions of years, the world must now be in the Seventh Period of its existence, according to the theory.

Now we shall compare the rock formations as required to meet the Genesis account, as aeons, with what is actually found. As, according to the speculation, there were no fossils of any kind possible until the close of the Third Period; all that preceded was entirely free from them. In other words, if plants, the first form of life, did not appear until that part of the Third Period which followed the appearance of land and sea, all that preceded this time belonged to the Azoic Era. This latter designation was given some time ago to the lowest formation which was believed to be free from life. This formation was largely an ideal based on the theory that at the time seemed well-founded. When it was tested out by exploration in the field, it was found that no such formation was in evidence. No sedimentary rock could be found so deep that it was entirely free

131

from evidence of fossils. Nor has it ever been possible to identify with certainty the primordial granite beneath. In field observation, fossil evidence of life is found as far down as sedimentary rock extends. When this was found to be true, the theory of an Azoic Era was dropped. The facts do not support it.

Yet the aeon-day speculation demands (1) two whole periods of it and part of a third. Furthermore, the speculation demands (2) that there be a clear dividing line between the First and Second, and between the Second and Third as well, for the words "And evening and morning were the first day" make a clear distinction between the close of the First Day and the beginning of the Second. A similar statement at the close of the Second Day marks its end, which is followed by the beginning of the Third Day. As the conditions for sedimentation continued the same through the first two periods, there was no possible physical mark of distinction between them. The speculation requires (3) that the sedimentary formations of both periods be of uniform, fine texture. The rock as actually found has nothing like this to correspond. These three objections are fatal to the speculation.

A further requirement of the speculation is (1) that animal fossils appear for the first time in the Fifth Period, and (2) that they be preceded by one entire Period and a part of another Period in which plant fossils appear alone. What is actually found is that animal fossils do not follow plant fossils occurring alone. The two are always intermingled. Nor do animal fossils first appear after more than half of geological time has passed. These are two more objections fatal to the speculation.

Many of the plants require insects to carry their pollen from flower to flower for fertilization, otherwise this class of plants would become extinct. As plants would have come into existence on the Third Period and animals on the Fifth, all of this class of plants would have perished for want of insects to carry their pollen. In the first place, (1) the fact that we still have this class of plants is proof that no such long period intervened between the first appearance of plants and animals.

Furthermore, (2) a God who would create in such an order as the speculation requires would not be a being of wisdom. Each day here assumed to be a Period was divided into two parts, an evening of darkness or night and a morning or daylight. If the Period following the plants had begun with a condition of darkness prevailing for many thousands of years, (3) all of the plants would have perished for want of light to sustain them. Then, (4) the animals of the Fifth Period would have had no food, and all would have died for lack of food as soon as they were created. And (5) man, when created on the Sixth Period, would have died also for lack of food. Again, a God who would have created such an order of things would not have been a being of wisdom. He could not possibly have been the God of the Bible. Here the speculation meets five more fatal objections.

The purpose of plants is to furnish food and shelter to animals and man. According to the speculation, plants existed during a part of one aeon and through all of two more aeons without serving their highest function, that of supplying food, shelter, and other benefits to man. All of this time they lived without a human eye to behold the beauty of their verdure and their flowers, or a mouth to feed upon their fruit. They existed, then, millions of years in vain and still more millions of years without serving their ultimate purpose. This would be most wanton waste. Why such prodigious waste of time and energy? Thus, there are still further objections which are fatal to the aeon-day speculation.

An aeon is a period of very great and also indefinite length. Therefore, if Adam was created in the Sixth Period considered as an aeon, it would be impossible (1) to determine his age in years. Yet the Bible gives his exact age in years. Furthermore, he would have lived through all the remainder of the Sixth Aeon, through the whole of the Seventh and through a portion of the time following. This (2) would make him millions of years old when he died. The Bible settles all this folly by stating that Adam was 930 years old when he died (Gen. 5:5). No one with any regard for the truth or for reason, to say nothing of the accuracy of the Bible, could indulge in this wholly groundless speculation. It leads to ridiculous results and directly contradicts the Bible. Here the speculation meets two more fatal objections.

According to the speculation, the period of man extended through a part of the Sixth Aeon and all of the Seventh; the latter, according to some who hold to the aeon speculation, is still going on. Man has been in existence, therefore, during one entire aeon and part of another. Yet all informed on the facts of science know that the total period of man's existence is far too short to be designated an aeon. This is one more fatal objection to the speculation.

According to the Genesis account, man did not sin until after the close of the Seventh Day. Hence, disorder could not appear in the world until after the close of Reconstruction Week. There should be no rending of the rocks as shown in the faults, or volcanic eruptions, or imperfections in the plants. And there would be no disease among the animals or man. Nor would there be any carnivorous animals. The speculation wholly disregards the many objections that are fatal to it.

The Seventh Day, according to Genesis, was the only day of the first week that received God's blessing. Hence, everything was perfect at least on this day. Those who hold to the aeon-day speculation claim, as they are compelled to do, that the Seventh Aeon is still continuing and that God is still resting.[29] According to this, it follows that all past time, of whatever length it be regarded, must end in a period (one-seventh of all past time in length) which is a time of perfection with the blessing of God upon everything. This would disregard sin entirely and make the present world a paradise. It is the climax of theistic evolution. Thus, it must be concluded that there are significant objections to the aeon-day speculation, any one of which is fatal to it.

---

[29] J.W. Dawson, The Origin of the World (London: Hodder and Stoughton, 1877), p. 130.

The real test of any speculation is that of applying it to facts to see if it is in harmony with them. This has just been done with the speculation that the days of Genesis are aeons of geological time. It is found that the speculation does not meet the facts at a single point. The assumption that the days of Genesis are ages is almost invariably called a theory rather than a hypothesis, because the stronger term is preferred. All attempt to uphold speculation with appealing terms instead of facts is in itself a serious reflection upon the speculation. In science hypothesis is the designation given to speculation that is supported by at least some facts gained from many tests. When supported by many facts, the speculation is designated a theory. The aeon-day speculation is not supported by even a single fact out of a large number of tests applied to it. This throws it out of the field of science entirely. Hence, an investigation of the scientific merits of the aeon-day speculation discloses the plain fact that it is neither theory nor hypothesis. The assertion that the days of Genesis are aeons is sheer fiction. (See Appendix A for further light involving the Hebrew words <u>Yom</u>, day, and <u>Olam</u>, aeon.) (See Fig. 12.1 below.)

Figure 12.1: ÆON-DAY GEOLOGY

Source: L. Allen Higley, <u>Science</u> <u>and</u> <u>Truth</u>, New York: Fleming H. Revell Co., 1940.

Time Period.	Rock Formation as Required To Agree With Period.
First Æon-Day. All Sea. No Land.	A world-wide ocean precludes all possibility of shore deposits, such as fine sediment, sand, gravel, pebbles, and shingle. The sediment possible would be derived from meteoric dust and meteorites. *No Fossils of Any Kind.*

Second Æon-Day. All Sea. No Land.	The world-wide ocean continued as during the First Æon-Day. The resulting rock formation would be the same also. *No Fossils of Any Kind.*
Third Æon-Day. Sea and Land. Plants.	Shore deposits and the resulting shale, sandstone, and conglomerate first appear, because of the first appearance of land and shore line. *The First Fossils Appear, Consisting of Plants Only.*
Fourth Æon-Day. Sea and Land. Plants.	Rock formations and fossils continues the same as begun in the Third Æon-Day.
Fifth Æon-Day. Sea and Land. Plants and Animals.	The rock formations and the plant fossils continues the same as during the Fourth Æon-Day, with *The First Fossils of Animals Added.*
Sixth Æon-Day. Sea and Land. Plants, Animals, and Man.	Rock formations and fossils continues the same as during the Fifth Æon-Day, with *The First Fossils of Man Added.*
Seventh Æon-Day. Sea and Land. Plants, Animals, and Man.	This Æon-Day must begin after the appearance of man. Man has not existed long enough to mark even the beginning of an Æon. When the Seventh Æon-Day becomes old enough to give a rock formation yielding fossils, it might be called an Æon, but not until that time.

THE ROCK FORMATIONS THAT ACTUALLY EXIST DO NOT AGREE WITH THE ABOVE IN ANY RESPECT. THE SPECUALTION THAT THE DAYS OF GENESIS ARE ÆONS HAS NOTHING WHATSOEVER IN GEOLOGY TO SUPPORT IT.

XIII

BEFORE THE FALL OF MAN
(Genesis 2:4-25)

"These are the generations of the heavens and of the earth when they were created, in the day that the Lord God made the earth and the heavens." (Gen. 2:4.) Here the word day means merely time. (See Appendix A.)

This passage, when read casually, as is very often done, seems confusing. It begins by mentioning the heavens before the earth and closes by mentioning the two in the reverse order. In one place it says that the heavens and the earth were created, and in the other it states that they were made. It speaks of the generations of the heavens and of the earth, yet there is but one heaven and earth. How is it all to be understood, especially as a summarized statement?

It is all plain enough if read on its own merit and in the light of the related passages. Very definite and brief statements are made. It refers to the time when the heavens and the earth were created, mentioning the heavens first. Then it refers to the time when the earth and the heavens were made, mentioning the earth first. To the latter statement it also connects the making of every plant of the field before it was in the earth and of every herb of the field before it grew. Then it adds that this took place before God had caused it to rain upon the earth, and before the creation of man (v.5).

When it mentions the creation of the heavens and the earth it mentions the heavens first because this is the order in which creation is spoken of in Genesis 1:1. And, as is shown elsewhere, there is good reason for believing that the heavens

137

were created before the earth.[30] Hence, "created" as used in Genesis 2:4 refers to Genesis 1:1. However, when the verse speaks of the making of the earth and the heavens, it names the earth first and then the heavens. This, again, corresponds with the previous account; for in the account of the first four days of Reconstruction Week, God made the earth first and then the heavens.

The making or reconstruction of the earth took place on the first three days, and that of the heavens: sun, moon, and stars, on the fourth day. It should be noted also that in this account (Gen. 1:3-19) the word create does not occur at all. It is made instead. Thus we know that Gen. 2:4, which speaks of the making of the earth and of the heavens, must refer to the reconstruction of the world and not its creation. In fact, considering only the natural world, we might better call the seven days Reconstruction Week instead of Creation Week, as explained in Chapter XII.

The passage commonly called the Fourth Commandment is not only clear evidence that the seven days of Genesis are literal,[31] but this period was a time of reconstruction necessitated by sin, not by primal creation. The fact that God made instead of created the physical world and what is in it is clear evidence of reconstruction.[32] The further fact that the acts of God are called work and are distributed over a period of time is additional proof of reconstruction. That man, after receiving the law through Moses in his fallen state, must limit his work to six days and his rest to one day in every seven is also proof that God was dealing with sin during the first seven days (Gen. 1:3-2:3).

The act of God at primal creation was instantaneous; the word "created" is used to record it; and it is not spoken of as work. It had nothing at all to do with sin. The context is not in any way in keeping with the fact of regulating the work and the

---

[30] See Chapters III and VIII.

[31] See Chapter XII; Exo. 20:8-11.

[32] See Chapters X and XI.

rest of man as a sinner, as given in the Fourth Commandment. The numerous acts of God in reconstruction, however, are fully in keeping with the Commandment.

Why should the word generation be used in the plural in the summary of Genesis 2:4 instead of in the singular, since it is all one world? The word generation means the order of the history of a thing. Let us consider the heavens and the earth in this respect. When they were first created, and before sin entered, they were in the first phase of their history. From the time of the first sin to the close of the great cataclysm they were in the second phase. The time from the beginning of the reconstruction which followed the cataclysm to its completion at the time of the creation of man, which was the event with which the summary ends, constituted the third phase of their history. Thus at least three phases or generations of the history of the heavens and of the earth are covered in the summarized statement of Genesis 2:4. The statement is highly accurate even in its details. It is fully in keeping with the inspiration.

The summary includes in what was made: the earth, and the heavens, and "every plant of the field and every herb of the field." This is in agreement with the previous account also (Genesis 1:3-31); but it states, in addition, that the plants were made before they were in the earth and before they grew. Thus, we are to understand that though they were not created anew, they were refashioned or reconstructed. (See Chapter VII.) The former plants that had been destroyed in the great cataclysmic judgment were not suited to the new order of things. They still bore the marks of the influence of sin; hence they had to be made over so that these traits would not be propagated in the new world that was to begin without sin.

At this time there was no rain upon the earth. Instead, there was a mist that rose and watered the whole face of the ground. These conditions for watering the ground so plants could grow were so different from the present conditions that we cannot fully understand them. The expression "there went up a mist from the earth, and watered the whole of the ground" reminds us

139

of the action of heavy dew. It must have been very much more than this, however, for there were waters, no doubt, above the firmament in great enough amount to cause a considerable part of the Flood that occurred later. Hence, the supply of moisture to the ground was comparatively large, and it was sufficient for plants to grow abundantly. It watered the whole face of the ground. There were no deserts and no swamps or rocky, nonproductive areas. The rocks were beneath the ground in the reconstructed earth. They have been uncovered since.

The summary gives some additional information regarding the creation of man. As to his body, he was formed (not created) out of the dust of the ground. (The dust of the ground was already in existence.) The life came from God. It did not come from the dust, nor from any animal. It came from God, who alone can create man's life. It was breathed into man's nostrils "the breath of life (lives—plural, Heb. Hayyim, the kind of life that goes on and on, eternal life), and man became a living soul" (v.7). Any other way of attempting to account for the origin of man is unscriptural, illogical, and foolish. In none of the so-called explanations of the origin of man through evolution is there an adequate cause for the result.

The newly created man was then placed in the garden that had been planted by the Creator (v.8). All we know about this garden is that it was located "eastward in Eden" and that it had plants and animals in it. Also that it was made to be the home of man. The name Eden is used here without introduction. The inference is that the region called by this name was in existence before. The garden was only a part of Eden, not the entire region, as is often erroneously assumed. The record states plainly that the garden was eastward in Eden. Since it was eastward in Eden, it could not have occupied the whole region called Eden.

The word Eden means delight, or place of pleasure. This place of delight, or pleasure, was larger than the garden located eastward in it. The garden is called also "the garden of Eden" (v. 15) after man was placed in it to dress and keep it. Because of this human interest to us we naturally call it by this term and usually overlook the fact that it was first called the "garden eastward in Eden" (v. 8). It was called by this name before man was placed in it. There are good reasons for concluding that the name Eden applied to the entire land area existing at this time, for it was all a delight.

Why should it be called by a somewhat different name here? The Genesis account does not explain this. We should naturally infer that man was not present when God planted the garden. Also that there was something connected with the history of it that was not to be revealed to man. The name Eden is also mentioned in Ezekiel 28:13; and 31:8, 9, although here it is designated "Eden the garden of God." Evidently, here, Eden was itself the garden and not just the east portion of the garden. "Eden the garden of God" was a larger place and more beautiful, we infer, than the "garden eastward in Eden" where man was placed. It contained no tree of knowledge of good and evil.

"Eden the garden of God" was the home of the ruler of the earth (Lucifer) before his fall. It is stated that he was "the sum, full of wisdom, and perfect in beauty." The Lord God said unto him: "Thou hast been in Eden the garden of God; every precious stone was thy covering, the ruby, topaz, and the diamond, the beryl, the onyx, and the jasper, the sapphire, the emerald, and the turquoise; and the gold, the workmanship of your settings and sockets was prepared in thee in the day that thou wast created. Thou wast the anointed cherub that covereth; and I placed thee so: thou wast upon the holy mountain of God; thou hast walked up and down in the midst of the stones of fire. Thou wast perfect in thy ways from the day that thou wast created, till iniquity was found in thee . . . thou hast sinned: therefore I will cast thee as profane out of the mountain of God: and I will destroy thee, O covering cherub, from the midst of the stones of fire. Thine heart was lifted up because of thy beauty, thou hast corrupted thy

141

wisdom by reason of thy brightness: I will cast thee to the ground." (Ezk. 28:12-17.)[33]

That his sin was pride caused by unholy ambition and disobedience is plainly shown in Isaiah 14:12-14 as follows: "How art thou fallen from heaven, O Lucifer, son of the morning! How art thou cut down to the ground, which didst weaken the nations! For thou hast said in thine heart, I will ascend into heaven, I will exalt my throne above the stars of God: I will sit also upon the mount of the congregation, in the sides of the north: I will ascend above the heights of the clouds,[34] I will be like the most High."[35]

He was the ruler of the earth, but he was not satisfied with this; for pride over his beauty entered his heart. It is clear that he had access to the garden of God with all of its beauty, and this undoubtedly was the place of his throne. After he sinned he had to be cast out. Then followed, after a period of unknown length, all of the judgment of destruction alluded to in Genesis 1:2.

The earth had to be reconstructed as the domain for man who was created to take the place of the fallen ruler. Man was placed in a garden also as the seat of his place of authority, though the record does not state that he had a throne. It would seem that the Garden eastward in Eden, the home of man, was located in the same place where the former "Eden the garden of God" had been. This seems a natural inference.

In any case, God who knew all things knew the entire past, including all its sin; but this He did not reveal to Adam for reasons of His own, which may easily be inferred. Adam was to be innocent of it all and to be protected from it by being given a single command and warning.

How far apart in time these two Edens were is nowhere revealed in the Scriptures. It represents the entire period of sin

---

[33] KJV and NASV.

[34] Exodus 19:9; 40:38; Nu. 16:42.

[35] II Thess. 2:4.

previous to man's time. The Scriptural evidence points toward a very long period. This is fully confirmed by science.

The garden eastward in Eden is described to some extent. God himself planted it and then placed man in it. It contained "every tree that is pleasant to the sight, and good for food; the tree of life also, and the tree of knowledge of good and evil." The tree of life gave to those who ate of it the power to live forever. It will again be found in the paradise of the new heaven and the new earth (Rev. 22:2). The nature of the tree of knowledge of good and evil is not stated, except by plain inference in connection with the fall of man. A river which watered the garden flowed out of Eden, parting into four heads. These are named Pison, Gihon, Hiddekel, and Euphrates. They watered the lands of Havilah, Assyria, and Ethiopia. These regions were probably in western Asia and northern Africa; we are not to assume, however, that the map of that time was the same as that of the present. Many things have taken place since to change it, among them the Flood.

Man was placed in the garden "to dress and to keep it" (v.15). His activity there was not called work; it was wholly a pleasure. His food was constantly and freely supplied. He was restricted by the single command, "But of the tree of the knowledge of good and evil, thou shalt not eat of it: for in the day that thou eatest thereof thou shalt surely die (dying, thou shalt die)." (Gen. 2:17.) These words of warning to man plainly imply that, if obedient, he would live forever. Verse 17 contains man's first intimation of evil. To Adam death was known only by word; to him it was a matter of future possibility only.

There, in the garden, man had his every want supplied. A blessing had been pronounced upon the man and the woman as soon as they were created. They had no knowledge of harm or of danger of any kind; not even a sense of shame or sin. They did not know that they were naked; nor had they knowledge of what it meant to be naked (v.25). They were in fact not naked in the real sense of the word; they were clothed with light. We know this from the fact that they were made in the image of God,

143

who is all light (Psalm 104:2). So long as they obeyed Him they partook of His nature, and light radiated from Him to clothe them. They were supremely happy.

They were, however, living under one law. And this made sin possible. "But sin is not imputed when there is no law." (Rom. 5:13.) Why, then, was the law given? God did not place the law over them to tempt them; "for God cannot be tempted with evil, neither tempteth He any man." (Jas. 1:13.) No, he loves His children, for "God is love." (I John 4:16.) We know that He placed the newly created pair under a law because He loved them. It was to be their protection against sin.

Sin had been in the world before and it brought about ruin. God knew that the reconstructed world, which He had just made, was subject to the entrance of sin. He knew that the devil, "who sinneth from the beginning" (I John 3:8), was still in existence and that he had access to the garden in which man dwelt. The one law, which God instituted, was the only thing essential to the lasting happiness of man. So He made the law as the only thing that would protect man under the conditions then prevailing. It was a complete protection, because man had the full power under free will to obey.

However, why did not God make man so He could not disobey? Because that would have made man an automaton, not capable of rulership in God's place. From every point of view, God treated man justly.

To Adam was given the naming of the animals, "and whatsoever Adam called every living creature, that was the name thereof " (v.19). This is the first recorded instance of man's exercise of free will. Many scientific men have taken exception to the Bible at this point, claiming that it was impossible for any one man to name all of the animals with their more than 700,000 species. This is an erroneous view, based on a very superficial knowledge of the Scriptures. The animals that Adam named were perfect in their differentiation between species. The animals of our time have been subject to modification and decline because of sin. Many that we call different species are

144

only varieties. In our taxonomy there is much needless repetition with new names.

The story is told of a young lady who decided to labor as a dock worker. She did heavy work as a machine operator who loaded and unloaded cargo from ships. The pay was good, and she did that work for several months. One morning she awoke to find hair growing on her chest. She promptly quit her job.

It seems the body compensates for the demands made upon it. Her male hormones had sprung into action from manual overload. A species can change (modify) within a species, but a species does not change into another kind of species. They are a different order of creation.

An analogy of the above story can be made in animals who begin to grow thicker fur when their environment becomes much colder than the climate they originally experienced. This does not constitute evolution. They are still of the same species; their accommodating modification produced a different variety of the same species.

Critics hasten to the conclusion that Adam was inferior to men today because of lack of training and experience. This is also of gross error. Men today are for the most part out of touch with God because of the sin in their ancestry for scores of generations. The world has become more sinful and hence more limited in intelligence with the passing of the centuries. Critics overlook this and also their own limitation because of sin. They forget that sin makes for stupidity, not for intelligence. This is especially true of the sin of rejecting Christ, who is the "Light of the world," and God's Word, which is a light unto man's path.

At the time Adam named the animals, he was a perfect man. His intellect was in the perfection of its power. He had neither sin of his own nor inherited sin. He came directly from his Creator, who was the essence of perfection. He spoke to God face to face. Who of us can claim even a small portion of all this? Adam was equal to naming all of the animals. "And Adam gave names to all cattle, and to the fowl of the air, and to every beast of the field; but for Adam there was not found an help meet for him." (Gen. 2:20.)

Adam's wife could not come from the animals, because they are a different order of creation. She had to be specially created. "All flesh is not the same flesh: but there is one kind of flesh of men, another flesh of beasts, another of fishes, and another of birds." (I Cor. 15:39.) Here is the authoritative statement to show that human flesh could not possibly come from animal flesh. Nor could one kind of animal come from another. This is fully confirmed by science in many ways. It is, therefore, incorrect to call man an animal. The proper terminology is "human being" or "creature" (that which is created).

The method of bringing the first woman into the world is given in Genesis 2:21, 22. The purpose was that she might be Adam's wife and intimate companion. Animals were not created with the gift of speech; hence man can never have the intimate companionship with them that goes with the exercise of this higher gift.

Evolution is one of the very worst of sinful speculations. It would have one believe its guesses regardless of the facts. Inability to understand is not the real cause of the rejection of special creation. It is sin. Such a person will have to say he will not understand. If one who rejects the Biblical account of the creation of woman could say that he himself is without sin, then he would have a right to a hearing; for the creation of the first woman was a sinless creation. Adam had not sinned, and there was no other human being in existence.

The purpose of the creation of the first woman was that marriage might be established. This institution was established when God said, "It is not good that the man should be alone; I will make him an help meet for him." (Gen. 2:18.) Then all the animals were made to pass before the man, not only that he might name them, but also to show him that none of them was suited to his need of intimate companionship. "But for Adam there was not found an help meet for him" (v. 20). Adam was made to feel the need of a wife before she was given to him. She was not imposed upon him. This is still the basis of true marriage. How long the happy pair lived in perfect bliss is not revealed. There is no intervening account. We infer that it was not long. A creature as full of sin as Satan would lose no time in bringing about the downfall of the sinless ruler who was ruling in his place.

XIV

THE FALL OF MAN
(Genesis 3:1-24)

"Now the serpent was more subtle (crafty) than any beast of the field which the Lord God had made. And he said unto the woman, Yea, hath God said, Ye shall not eat of every tree of the garden?" (Gen. 3:1.)

We cannot fully realize the meaning of the word <u>subtle</u> as used here. From what is stated we may easily understand that of all the animals God made, the serpent was the most like a human being. It walked upright. At least we should infer this from the curse pronounced upon it after man's fall (v. 14). It must have been the most beautiful for the same reason. Its human resemblance must have been strong or it could not have been used to speak words readily understood by the woman.

Was it a mere serpent as such that spoke to the woman? No, animals do not have the power of speech. This animal spoke by some other power than its own. Otherwise, as an ordinary animal, it could not have spoken at all. Where, we ask, did the power come from? It came from Satan, who used the beast as his means of communicating with the woman. The speech was his, though it appeared to be that of the attractive serpent. He caused it to appear to the woman that this beast was the most beautiful and intelligent of all the animals. It seems that Satan caused the beast to appear to her more attractive than her husband, and so she heeded the appeal.

Why did Satan thus speak to the woman rather than to the man? This we may only infer. Perhaps it was because she was willing to consider some other creature more desirable than her husband. Some women are still led into sin through a similar snare. Perhaps it was partly because Satan knew that she had not been told directly not to eat of the fruit, but only indirectly

148

through her husband; and thus she would not be as fully impressed with the need of heeding God's command. Perhaps it was also due partly to the fact that she was the weaker vessel (I Pet. 3:7) and that she would be for that reason more easily deceived.

Satan's sin was that of questioning God's definitely stated word. "Yea, hath God said?" are the first recorded words of sin. The impressive thing here is that questioning God's word is in itself sin and that it leads others to sin.

It is not easy for us to imagine just what was the nature of the impression that the voice of the serpent had upon Eve when she first heard it. It is impossible for us to put ourselves in her place. We can understand a measure, perhaps, for we know how a beautiful animal appeals to us. This animal, however, spoke like a human being. No other animal could do this. Nor had this animal spoken before. What impression would such a thing make on one of us? To hear an animal speak like a person! That would be a perversion of what God has created. Therefore, not an attraction to us but a horrible thing!

The woman listened to the question and, instead of rejecting it, replied, "We may eat of the fruit of the trees of the garden: But of the fruit of the tree which is in the midst of the garden, God hath said, Ye shall not eat of it, neither shall ye touch it, lest ye die (vv. 2 and 3). In quoting God's command, she added "neither shall ye touch it." God had not said this. In the Scriptures we are forbidden to add anything to them. We are fully warned against this. There is no record, however, that she had such warning.

She, of course, did not have the Bible as we have. If God did not forbid her adding to His Word, it was not sin for her to do so; though it encouraged the sin of the one who tempted her. Satan now became emboldened and said to her, "Ye shall not surely die" (v. 4). This was a flat contradiction of God's word. The sin of questioning God's word leads directly to the additional sin of contradicting it. This is what evolution and similar speculation does.

149

Then Satan went on to say, "For God doth know that in the day ye eat thereof, then your eyes shall be opened, and ye shall be as gods, knowing good and evil" (v. 5). Satan did not say that he himself knew that this would be the result of her eating the forbidden fruit. Instead of having her believe it on his own word, he wanted her to believe it on the authority of God. This was the magnitude of his deceit. Neither did he tell her that God can know evil without experiencing it, but man has to experience evil to know it.

Had the woman shown wisdom, she would have taken the matter to God for the light she needed. He had created her and her husband and had given her food, a home, and every blessing. She knew that all she had in the world came from God. Now that a new thing came to her, especially one involving disobedience to her Creator, she should have gone to Him for help.

Instead of doing this, she did what has become so common ever since: she acted on her own judgment without consulting God, or even her husband, and did this in the presence of the one who was tempting her.

She looked at the tree and saw that its fruit was good for food, but forgot God's warning and the fact that already she had an abundance of food. She saw that it was pleasant to the eyes, but forgot the many other beautiful trees of the garden that God had provided for her pleasure. She was now giving her whole attention to just this one tree. She saw also that it was a tree to be desired to make one wise; she forgot that her Creator was the All Wise One who supplies His children with needed wisdom. This was a kind of wisdom that God had withheld from her. She should have felt some concern for the outcome if she should partake of it. And then "she <u>took</u> the fruit thereof," forgetting again that her food had been <u>given</u> to her (Gen. 1:29), and that <u>it</u> <u>should</u> <u>not</u> <u>be</u> <u>taken</u>. Now that she had touched the forbidden food, she was ready for the final and sinful act, "and did eat" (v. 6).

150

She disobeyed God, violated her conscience, and, of course, experienced a change in her nature. She now loved herself more than God. She also loved herself more than her husband. She offered him the forbidden fruit because she wanted him to be like herself. Had she loved him more than herself, she would have warned him against disobedience.

When it was given to him, he was not obliged to eat it. He saw the result that eating it had upon his wife. She was no longer the kind of wife God had given him. She was now a sinner and had a sinner's nature. Her offer of the forbidden food to him after she had eaten of it was the proof that she loved herself more than him. He had to make his choice now between obeying God and heeding his sinful wife. He knew that she sinned through deception, but he was not deceived (I Tim. 2:14). He saw the effect it had upon her. Yet, deliberately "he did eat."

It was neither the man nor the woman who was the originator of sin. Their record was the beginning of sin of the human race. The woman committed the first sin through being deceived. The second sin was by the man, done deliberately. She heeded the serpent instead of God. He listened to his wife. Both of them held Satan's lie above the Word of God. It brought upon them and upon their off-spring the sentence of death. Satan had told the woman that she would not surely die. That was partly true and thus a deception, the worst form of lie. She did not die at once, but gradually through a period of years ("dying, thou shalt die" is the Hebrew rendition in Gen. 2:17).

Just what kind of food was it? Could it have been food in a figurative sense? It is dangerous to introduce figures of speech into the Bible unnecessarily. This is the first step in undermining God's Word. It introduces speculation. Where figurative language is used the context always makes this clear. Here the context indicates that it is literal. The other trees bore literal fruits to be used as literal food. God recognized the possibility of their eating this fruit also if not warned. He made no other distinction between the two kinds of fruit than the one that this

151

fruit would cause their death. They did eat it, and they did die. Hence, we may reasonably conclude that it was a literal food.

Then what kind of fruit was it? In the light of all of the circumstances, we might conclude that it was a poisonous fruit from the former plant world before Reconstruction Week. We note that when God planted the garden (2:9) the record does not state that He created the tree of knowledge of good and evil. Nor could He have done so, because it was an evil plant, and He does not create any evil thing. It, therefore, must have been due to sin. The only sin that had ever been in the world before this was that previous to the time of man's creation. Hence, the evil in this one plant came from the preAdamic world of sin. It had never been remedied in the sense of having been done away with entirely. Satan, the cause of it, was still alive and active, even on the earth; for it was possible for him to enter an animal and also to enter man.

Since pre-Adamic sin was due to disobedience, and sin was still in the world, it would obviously follow that Adam's price of safety was obedience. Satan knew this and so sought to reach Adam through Eve.

Let us consider the possible reason that food was made the object for man's temptation. Man's eternal life requires spiritual food, the bread of life. "Verily, verily, I say unto you, Moses gave you not that bread from heaven; but my Father giveth you the true bread from heaven. For the bread of God is He which cometh down from heaven, and giveth life unto the world." (John 6:32, 33.) This bread was Jesus. He is typified in this by the literal bread of the Lord's Supper.

The natural body required natural food for its life. Adam's natural life, as long as he did not sin, would continue eternally; but his natural body required natural food. Of course, his sinless body required a food in no way connected with sin. His sinless, natural body required the natural food that God had made for it, and this would be a food not contaminated through the result of sin. A food from a plant contaminated because of the curse of sin would act as a poison and introduce into the natural body the elements of death, working gradually until finally the body would die. At the same time, in the spiritual sense, the mere act of disobedience to God would cause separation from Him which is spiritual or eternal death; for the spirit has eternal existence.

This, it would seem is the explanation of how death came upon man. His act of disobedience caused his spiritual death at once. He was created to be in intimate touch with God. His love for God had to be shown by keeping God's commandment; and this divine principle is still true: "If ye love me, keep my commandments." (John 14:15.) Eating a forbidden food would result in taking into the natural body the elements which would eventually cause death. The forbidden food was the bread of Satan. It separated Adam and Eve from the Bread of Life.

As soon as Adam and Eve sinned, they lost their innocency and with it the light that clothed them. Feeling the sense of shame, they covered themselves with aprons made of fig leaves. This was only the appearance of a real remedy. Each one still retained the sense of shame. It has been so ever since. No vain imagination or foolish philosophies can ever remove it, in spite of the repeated and brazen efforts through the centuries, especially recently. Man cannot change God's plan of creation.

They tried first to cover up their shame and then to hide from God. This is still the way of the sinner. But God knows all things. There is nothing hidden from Him. He called Adam first; for Adam was the head of the home. He was the one who had sinned deliberately. The voice of God made him afraid. "There is no fear in love; but perfect love casteth out fear; because fear hath torment. He that feareth is not made perfect in love" (I John 4:18.) His fear, then, was the proof of his lack of love for God. Since those who love God keep His commandments, it is obvious that Adam had not loved God. And the first searching question he had to face was, "Hast thou eaten of the tree, whereof I commanded thee that thou shouldest not eat?"

Adam answered by blaming his wife. Naturally so, for he now loved himself more than he loved her. Thus we see that sin had the same effect upon both of them. Then God spoke to the woman. She answered by blaming the serpent. Neither one took upon himself the responsibility for disobedience. They both sought self-justification.

We do not see their sad plight as we should, because being sinners ourselves, we have to see it from the sinners' standpoint. Their sin cost them their lives. Therefore, it cost them everything. Their life had been one of the greatest joy. Every need was supplied. They knew only bliss. They were wholly innocent of every evil. Just a single law to keep (Gen. 2:17), and they were fully endowed with the power to keep it; otherwise, they would not have been held responsible for obedience. Keeping the law was wholly a matter of their own free will unhindered by anything external.

Obedience was really a test of their love for God, who gave them everything they had, and to whom they owed everything. The debt of love for God was wholly their own. Yet, when the hour of temptation came, they forgot the debt and its required obedience. Instead, they took their blessings for granted, just as has been done ever since by their followers in sin. They had no justification whatsoever for disobedience.

God's sentence followed immediately. It was not one of wrath on God's part; for His Word nowhere states that it was. It was an act of mercy. He had created a world of righteousness in the beginning and later reconstructed it on the plan of righteousness again because that was the only thing He could do. Nothing else would endure. Now that Adam and Eve's sin had brought destruction into the world, He as their loving Father must tell them what the result would be.

God judged the creatures in order: The serpent first, then the woman, and lastly the man. To the serpent God said, "Because thou hast done this, thou art cursed above all cattle, and above every beast of the field; upon they belly shalt thou go, and dust shalt thou eat all the days of thy life (v. 14): And I will put enmity between thee and the woman, and between thy seed and her seed; it shall bruise they head, and thou shalt bruise his heel"

(v. 15; Rev. 12:9). Today, the serpent is cursed apart from any beast. It crawls upon its belly and eats dust with its food. There is enmity between it and man. The next part of the curse appears to be inflicted upon the evil spirit indwelling the beast, rather than upon the beast as such. That it extended further than the beast itself is clearly shown by the prophecy that the seed of the woman would bruise the serpent's head, and that the serpent would bruise the heel of the woman's seed. This refers without doubt to the long conflict then beginning between Satan and man.

To the woman God said, "I will greatly multiply thy sorrow and thy conception; in sorrow (pain) thou shalt bring forth children; and thy desire shall be to thy husband, and he shall rule over thee" (v. 16). There is always a relationship between sin and its consequences. It is the relationship between cause and effect. By examining an effect we learn something of the cause. The results were: (1) enmity between her and the serpent; (2) multiplied sorrow and conception; (3) bringing forth children in sorrow; (4) desire unto her husband, and (5) that he should rule over her.

The first result indicates that the cause was improper friendship; the second and third, that she had extended the family joy of conversation to include a beast. She had spoken to it as to a member of her family. Yet she knew that her husband was the only creature around her with the gift of speech. When she heard the serpent speak, she knew that such speech was a perversion and that it should have been rejected. Instead, she entertained it. This was a perverted extension of her family circle. Hence, her true family circle would be a sorrowful one. The last two results of her sin show that she was not content with being her husband's helpmate but went ahead of him independently in her relation with the serpent. She had gone away from him; now her desire must be unto him. She thought she did not need him when she spoke to the serpent; but now she would find herself dependent upon him. She went ahead of him in eating the forbidden fruit and then led him to eat also, instead

155

of acting as his helpmate. She tried to be the leader; and now she would have to submit to his rule over her. (See Appendix B.)

"And unto Adam He said, Because thou hast hearkened unto the voice of thy wife, and hast eaten of the tree, of which I commanded thee, saying, Thou shalt not eat of it: cursed is the ground for thy sake; in sorrow shalt thou eat of it all the days of thy life. Thorns also and thistles shall it bring forth to thee; and thou shalt eat of the herb of the field. In the sweat of thy face shalt thou eat bread, till thou return unto the ground; for out of it wast thou taken: for dust thou art, and unto dust shalt thou return" (vs. 17-19).

He had eaten forbidden food to gratify a false pleasure. He, through his wife, had taken a food from one who had no right to it, instead of receiving his food as a gift from God. (See Gen. 129.) His failure to appreciate his free gift would render it no longer a free gift. He would have to work for it. He had taken the forbidden food to satisfy his false pleasure. Now his true food would be obtained in sorrow and also eaten in sorrow. Besides, it would result finally in his death.

The man was first spoken of by the name Adam (the man) at the time he named the animals. This was before he yielded to sin. His name is used without introduction. We do not know how he received his name. Perhaps he named himself before he named the animals. He called his helpmate woman ("woman, because she was taken out of man"). God made her from a rib taken out of Adam's side (2:21, 22). After both had sinned, "Adam called his wife's name Eve, because she was (became)[36] the mother of all living" (3:20). "It was through the power of divine grace that Adam believed the promise with regard to the

---

[36] See footnote number 49.

woman's seed, and manifested his faith in the name which he gave to his wife."[37]

"Unto Adam also and to his wife did the Lord God make coats of skins, and clothed them" (v. 21). This was while they were still in the garden and after they had sinned. Their fig leaves were insufficient to cover their shame in a manner acceptable to God. God knew that their clothing must be made of something which would signify sin, the reason for their shame.

Plucked leaves did not signify anything wrong. There was no mark of sin in plucked fig leaves. Adam and Eve's sin had cost life for themselves and for all their posterity. And the life is in the blood (9:4). "For the life of the flesh is in the blood." (Lev. 17:11.) Therefore, their sin had cost blood. They had to be clothed with skins instead of leaves. Nothing else would satisfy divine justice. Man has been wearing skins and furs in one form or another ever since. Civilized man tans the skins, dresses them up to make them look attractive, and calls them leather of some particular kind. Furs of various kinds are in constant demand as apparel and are worn especially by women. The essential thing to observe is that all furs and skins bear the mark of sin. It is a bloody and disagreeable mark which cannot be removed by processes of civilization. It is true that we wear leather for protection and comfort; but Adam and Eve wore skins merely for decency. They did not need any protection from cold or anything else, for they were still in the garden, the paradise of God.

Having free will and being under sin, Adam and Eve faced the possibility of eating of the tree of life in the garden and living forever (v. 22). For their own sakes God could not permit them to do this. If man should live forever in a state of sin he would suffer still greater calamity than death. "Therefore, the Lord

---

[37] Keil and Delitzsch, <u>Biblical Commentary on the Old Testament</u> (Grand Rapids: Eerdmans Publ. Co., 1912), p. 106.

God sent him forth from the garden of Eden. . . . So he drove out the man" (3: 23, 24). They were apparently sent out, but were reluctant to go and had to be driven out. A guard was placed at the entrance to the garden to protect the tree of life from them (v. 24). This plainly shows that man naturally clings to his life and wants to live forever even in a state of sin. His sin does not remove his desire to live; he was created to live forever, and this desire remains with him. It is still true today. No one welcomes death as such. Those who say they long to die really do not long for death for its own sake, but for the advantages which they believe it will bring them.

Thus ended man's time in the garden eastward in Eden. While he was there, he was perfectly happy as long as he obeyed. His remaining there and also his happiness were conditioned on obedience to a single command. Everything he had was a free gift from God, to whom he owed everything. He had produced nothing himself; hence, he could claim nothing in his own right. All that he had was a gift of love from God. He lost his gift through failure to show in return enough love to his benefactor and Creator to obey Him. He could no longer live there. Really, he had no right to live at all under any conditions.

God's infinite love, however, would not have it so. He had made man in His own image (1:26), and He could not let him go to his deserved fate. Upon his profession of faith in Christ as Saviour, He would create man a new creature that would finally be placed in a new heaven and a new earth. There, in that new world forever free from sin, the new man will live and reign with God forever and ever. (II Cor. 5:17; John 1:12.)

Man's sin necessitated that the work involved in his redemption be done by stages or processes. As a free-will being, man needs time in which to make his choice. The result will fully justify the way of bringing it about. When the Infinite God creates a being like unto Himself, a finite period of time is required. When the task shall have been fully completed, then time shall be no more. All the redeemed will dwell in eternity.

XV

THE SUSTENANCE OF MAN
(The Food Question)

Food is important because it is necessary to maintain the physical strength of the body. If not properly selected, food may become a cause of disease. Thus food is of vital concern to everyone.

Food influences also the mind and the spirit. In this aspect it becomes closely related to sin and may indeed become a contributory cause of sin. For the guidance of all, the Bible contains very definite statements on food. These statements are seldom taken seriously by unbelievers. They are often neglected by believers. The latter often take the view that there is no relation between food and living the separated life. Hence, they follow the customs of the unbeliever and seem to feel entirely satisfied with it, especially as long as they are well. When illness comes they are more open to a consideration of better foods and better habits of eating, especially if health is not soon regained. Upon recovery some seem to profit for a time from the lessons of illness caused by wrong food. The great majority, however, return to their old habits of eating, vainly hoping that in some way they will acquire resistance to ward off further trouble.

Let us turn to the Bible as the authority and learn what it states regarding food. And let us hope that we shall find the truth that is so often neglected through failure to use the Bible, or through a false interpretation of its teaching on this subject.

I. Food Under Sinlessness

First of all, what was man's food in his sinless condition, and to what extent does he still eat the same food? "Behold, I have

159

given you every herb bearing seed, which is upon the face of all the earth, and every tree, in the which is the fruit of a tree yielding seed; to you it shall be for meat (food)." (Gen. 1:29.) From this authority we know that originally man's food was seed, or grain, and the fruit of every plant in the entire world. Man's food came from the plants that had been ordered on the third day. We note the words "every herb" and "every tree"; the fruit of each one was given for food. From this we know that there were no poisonous plants at that time. We should know this also from the fact that these plants had just been ordered through the direct command of God. He could not have brought into being poisonous plants at any time. (See Chapters VII and X.)

This condition would have continued indefinitely if sin had not followed. Man in his natural body required natural food; yet he would have lived forever if he had not sinned. This was the original plan for man. He still feels instinctively that it is natural to live and unnatural to die; he enjoys life and shuns death.

II. Food Under the Curse

"And when the woman saw that the tree was good for food, and that it was pleasant to the eyes, and a tree to be desired to make one wise, she took the fruit thereof, and did eat, and gave also unto her husband with her; and he did eat." (Gen. 3:6.)

The very first sin of the human race entered through the eating of forbidden food. The warning had been given, "But of the tree of the knowledge of good and evil, thou shalt not eat of it: for in the day that thou eatest thereof thou shalt surely die."[38] The warning came from the creator to whom man owed every thing he had in the whole world. The circumstances leading to the failure to obey are given in Genesis 3:1-5. This was taken up in Chapter XIV.

---

[38] ("dying, thou shalt die." Gen. 2:17.)

Let us inquire somewhat into the immediate effect sin had upon the body. Since it brought sickness and ultimately death itself, it defiled the body. This defilement resulted in God's making a change in man's food, for now the <u>herb</u> of the field was added (Gen. 3:18). Defilement came not only from sin but from the guilt of sin. A guilty conscience has a defiling effect on the body. The eating of the forbidden fruit led to other disobedience, and it all resulted in defiling the body. It is a fact today that the human body is not only greatly defiled in general, but particularly in its entire alimentary tract. In fact, this defilement is so great that it is not proper to dwell on the subject. The vital thing is that it all resulted from sin in eating. The defilement is the effect of the sin.

The disobedience brought also the sense of shame to both the man and the woman. The woman's disobedience brought to her multiplied sorrow and conception, and sorrow in bringing forth children. Man, in yielding to temptation, brought a curse upon himself also. He had to share her burden of sin in addition to his own.

Of course, the calamity resulting from sin did not all come in a moment. It came gradually as sin increased. The first sin was only the beginning of the long series of disasters consequent upon it. Serious as Adam's sin was, he lived nevertheless 930 years before his sin finally took him out of this world. In our time the average man goes to the grave before he has reached one-thirteenth of that age.

Thus we see in a general way the consequences of the first sin. It was so great a sin that the results cannot be fully comprehended. What should impress us is both the fact of sin and the cause of it. <u>It</u> <u>came</u> <u>through</u> <u>disobedience</u> <u>in</u> <u>eating</u>. Eating, not the wrong kind of food, for it was fruit; but the wrong thing of the right kind, for it was forbidden.

In the light of God's Word, what utterly blind presumption it is to say, as some do, that what we eat today has little or nothing to do with sin. Or to say that we may eat anything that appeals to the eye or tastes good. This is the very way sin began, although it resulted, nevertheless, in a longevity of nearly a thousand years. Shall we who have a longevity of very much less than that set up our foolish judgment in opposition and try to claim that what we eat does not matter so long as it tastes good?

Man is led to this sinfully presumptuous conclusion under the influence of the very same serpent that beguiled Eve in the first place. His first temptation was for the purpose of destroying the human race: spirit, soul, and body. Already he has reduced the span of life to a mere fraction of what it was after the first sin. Shall we allow him to reduce it still more by our willful disobedience? Shall we insist on our ways in spite of the lesson God is trying to teach us through His Word?

III. Food After the Flood

The disobedience that occurred in the matter of eating from the time of the first sin to the Flood is not revealed. We may infer, however, that there was a very great disobedience in this matter, though, of course, in other matters also (Gen. 6:3, 5-7). The result of it all was that the whole world had to be destroyed by a flood. This was the best thing under the circumstances, otherwise God would not have ordered it. Of the entire human race, only Noah and seven members of his family were preserved through the Flood. Though preserved they were, nevertheless, still sinners. Some of their kindred were among those who were so wicked that they had to be destroyed. This inheritance of sin was in the blood of those preserved. Hence, they were more deeply under sin than were our first parents, Adam and Eve.

This fact is indicated by the food given to them at this time. They were given the green herb, and the animal flesh that had the blood removed from it. They were still allowed, of course, to eat grain, fruit, and the herb of the field, just as Adam and Eve were after they had sinned. The diet was extended after the Flood to include inferior foods, <u>the</u> <u>green</u> <u>herb,</u> <u>and</u> <u>animal</u> <u>flesh</u> (Gen. 9:3).

Animal flesh was much inferior to grain and fruit because it was relatively an impure food, even at its best. The blood, which was expressly forbidden, was certain to remain in the meat to some extent as a contamination. Furthermore, the provision for this kind of food involved the shedding of blood, which meant suffering. This was unnatural to man because he was created to eat food not requiring the shedding of blood. He was created a vegetarian; now he must be partly carnivorous. This was against his original nature, and it is still that way. The added food was in keeping only with man's acquired nature under added sin. Of course, sin must pass away before man can be restored to full favor with God. With the passing of sin, the food prescribed for him under sin will have to pass away also.

Both clean and unclean animals were taken into the ark (Gen. 7:2). Man was probably left to his own judgment in the selection of his food from among these animals, just as is still the case in his selection of grain or of seed or of fruit. Whether he used good judgment or bad was dependent obviously upon whether he was under bondage to sin. Just after the Flood clean animals were seven times as abundant as unclean ones (Gen. 7:2). For this reason man would be more likely to select clean animals for his food. Besides, since man's memory of the Flood was still vivid, it is quite certain that he would associate unclean animals with sin, and so he would select the clean animals for his food. He had abundant reason to fear sin and everything associated with it.

After the Flood God merely added to what He had already given under the previous dispensation. Nothing was withdrawn.

IV. Food Under the Law

It was evident that sin increased rapidly after the Flood, and with the increase of sin diet degenerated. In fact, sin has increased ever since the first sin. Eve did not cease to sin after she sinned the first time by eating the forbidden fruit. She sinned again by offering it to her husband. Neither she nor her husband ceased to sin upon their expulsion from the garden. Nor did the children profit from their parents' experience; man only plunged deeper into the very cause of his ruin.

After all (except Noah and the other seven of his family who were with him in the ark) were destroyed by the Flood, Noah also followed after the things of the world. Man simply would not return to God of his own accord. Through his son, Shem, came a special man, Abraham, that God chose to be the father of a great people. Abraham's faith in God did not waver, and God blessed him. This people (Israel) multiplied greatly. From them came God's chosen prophet, Moses, who gave them the Divine law against sin.

At the same time God gave them special commands regarding their food. These commands are sometimes called the Dietary Laws of Moses, although this expression does not occur in the Bible. The chosen people called to the holy work of ministering salvation from sin were given the Dietary Laws before entering upon their work in the Holy Land.

There must have been a reason for this. By this time sin had spread so fast that man, no doubt, was eating all sorts of unclean food. A holy people could not remain holy without a regulated diet. Even in our own time it is well recognized that our diet has a great influence on our mental and on our spiritual condition. This is so well known that every one who ministers to the sick in any helpful way must be guided by an adequate knowledge of food.[39]

Every one in Israel, God's chosen people for the task, was in a sense a minister. They all had to work together to render the needed service. Those entrusted with the special work of the priesthood, or the ministry as we call it today, had to have the co-operation of the whole people in order to accomplish their work. God saw fit to prescribe the diet for all Israel because it

---

[39] See Deut. 29:6; Luke 1:15, and other passages.

was necessary for their spiritual welfare as well as for their health and strength.

We will now briefly examine the restrictions imposed by the Dietary Laws of Moses. Among the common land animals, those which parted the hoof and chewed the cud were good for food (Lev. 11:2, 3; Deut. 14:4-6); among the aquatic animals, those having fins and scales (Lev. 11:9; Deut. 14:9); among birds, the clean fowls (Deut. 14:11). As a further limitation, all blood of any animal was forbidden (Lev. 17:10-12); also the blood of "any beast or fowl that may be eaten" (Lev. 17:13, 14). Thus the blood of all animals was forbidden, even that of those whose flesh was given for food. Animals that died a natural death and those that were torn by beasts were forbidden for food (Lev. 17:15). The reason given for limiting animal food to the animals named was that all the others were unclean and an abomination. The blood was forbidden because it is the life (Gen. 9:4; Lev. 3:17; 17:14). Unclean animals are not fit for food because their flesh is defiled with impurities. Those defiled the most are especially unclean and are specifically mentioned: the hare, the swine, the eagle, and the vulture (Lev. 11:6-8, 13, 14; Deut. 14:12-19). Blood contains many of the impurities that must be eliminated from the system. It is injurious.

The animals given for food are the ones least affected by the curse that resulted from man's sin, also those having the best digestive system and the best elimination. Animals that have more than one stomach are in the latter class. Cattle have three stomachs and sheep, five. Fish with fins and scales have the best elimination among animals of their class. Animals that have died a natural death retain normally all of the blood in their flesh, and are possibly diseased also. Those torn by beasts would not be bled properly; and their struggles in mortal combat would result in imperfect elimination. Their flesh would be contaminated.

In every case the reason for forbidding the food was given. It was unclean and an abomination. Some of the reasons are plainly evident to us in our own time. It should be noted that no

165

animal of sea or land that is of the scavenger class is given for food. Nor is any carnivorous animal permitted for food. Both scavengers and carnivorous animals are in the class of those that have been affected the most by the fall of man. They have departed the farthest in their food from what was originally given to them, namely, the green herb (Gen. 1:30). As a sinner, man is under the sentence of death. His food is for the purpose of prolonging his life. It naturally follows that the food least affected by man's sin will prolong his life the most; those affected the most by sin will shorten his life the most.

To assert that one may violate this rule with impunity is equivalent to asserting that one evil is a remedy for another. This false principle has deceived many. It is deceiving many of God's children today. A common example of this is the assertion that poisonous drugs are a real remedy for disease.

Man's diseases are due to his sins and finally result in death (Gen. 3:19). Poisonous plants are also a result of sin (Gen. 3:18). One result of sin can never be a remedy for another. The principle in the use of mineral poisons is similar. God's Word does not in any place give minerals as such for man's food. Man obtains the minerals he needs through the food which were given him. The use of vegetable and mineral poisons as remedies for disease originated with the heathen. Sinlessness alone is the remedy for sin. God alone, who permitted sin to enter the world, understands it and has the remedy for it. All attempts to go ahead of Him are futile.

In every instance where God has placed restrictions upon man's food there is a very good reason, whether we can discover it scientifically or not. God requires first of all, obedience. Understanding is a matter for later consideration. Man in his innocency had but a single law to obey. It affected his eating. No explanation was given him as to the reason for the law, except that disobedience would result in death. Man was to obey, and not to understand beyond the reason stated to him. He was not told just how death would come to him, nor what the experience would be while passing on to his death. Obedience was God's first requirement.

One of man's great failings is that he does not wish to obey for the sake of obeying. Since the time of the first sin, man is naturally disobedient. He even tries to make excuses for his disobedience. One of the chief of these excuses is that he must understand first. This is in reality a manifestation of his sin, for he is incapable of understanding anything beyond that which God reveals to him. Man does not know the real nature of matter of any kind, nor of the phenomena it manifests. The chemistry involved in the change of his food into a part of his living body is a thing that man does not now understand and never will in the present life.

God restricted man's diet for the sake of his health, not for the sake of his salvation. He restricted his diet for the sake of his spiritual welfare also. The first sin in eating affected man spiritually. The effect of eating and drinking has never been changed. In confirmation of this, observe that in Isaiah 7:15 it was prophesied of the Lord that when He should come in the flesh, He would eat butter and honey "that he may know to refuse the evil, and choose the good." In Luke 1:15, where the birth of John the Baptist is predicated, it states "that he shall be great in the sight of the Lord, and shall drink neither wine or strong drink; and he shall be filled with the Holy Ghost, even from his mother's womb." These and other passages show that food and drink have a direct effect on the spiritual condition. Man cannot be filled with the Holy Spirit to do his best work unless he abstains from forbidden food and drink. This applied not only to John the Baptist, but also to Jesus, as man. John the Baptist, though Spirit-filled even from birth, evidently had to abstain in order to retain his Spirit-filled condition.

The children of Israel were chosen to be God's messengers to the world. They were to be a holy people. To maintain this state it was necessary for Israel to abstain from certain foods which God knew were harmful and which would defeat them in their high calling. This is clearly stated in Leviticus 11:44-47.

The same conditions have prevailed ever since. Man has never been able to set these laws aside without paying the price. The price must be paid in bad health and in spiritual decline. The history of Israel abundantly proves this. When Israel was faithful and obedient to God, they prospered. When they disobeyed they suffered. The one thing in which Israel never succeeded very long was the living of a life of separation from the world about them. The history of Israel is one long series of failures, followed at times by repentance and doing better for a limited time. Finally, when their disobedience became too great, they were captured by their enemies and had to go into exile.

In closing the comment on Foods Under Law, we should observe that here also no food given under any previous dispensation was withdrawn. The former foods were still to be continued.

V. Food Under Grace

We shall now consider food given under the dispensation of Grace. God still has His chosen people whom He blesses, though they live in a midst of a wicked world. The conditions for living in such an environment remain much the same as they were. Why should not the food be the same? Food that was good for Israel, the chosen people under Law, would be the best also for the followers of Jesus, under Grace.

No food condemned under Law was ever at any time sanctioned under Grace. The reason for this is clear. God who is the same "yesterday, and today, and forever" cannot bless under Grace what He condemned under Law and still be God. This would be placing His approval upon sin and its consequences.

That which was forbidden on the ground of being unclean must continue to be forbidden as long as it remains unclean. Nowhere in the Bible do we find the statement that the unclean

168

animals were cleansed at any time under Grace, or that they are to be cleansed during this time.[40] Their cleansing will not take place until the cause of the defilement is removed, namely, sin. The cleaning of the unclean and defiled animals will not take place until the Millennium.[41]

Faithful Christians are even more fully God's chosen people and, therefore, His holy people under Grace, than Israel ever was under Law. Under Grace, God expects and rightly requires a fuller obedience than He ever did under Law (Matt. 5:28f). Under Law, sin was covered by offering sacrifices as the Law required. Under Grace, we go directly to the Son who was sacrificed once for all for our sins. Yet, under Grace, we are expressly forbidden to sin that grace may abound (Rom. 6:15, 18).

Since food comes from God,[42] it is He, and not the world, that has the right and the wisdom to say what His children shall eat. He alone knows what is best.

Before the Flood there had been but one thing forbidden as food, and that was the fruit of the tree of the knowledge of good and evil (Gen. 2:17); after man sinned by disobeying, he was removed from that temptation (Gen. 3:23, 24). So, from Eden to the Flood, man was not exposed to the temptation of eating anything that had been forbidden. He could use his own judgment in the selection of food. Under the favorable climate of that time there was not the great number of poisonous plants nor of defiled animals that there is now. Under such a climate desirable food was much more easily obtained than at present. Should we conclude that after the Flood such beasts as we have now were eaten? No, for the conditions were not the same then as at present.

---

[40] See point VI this chapter.

[41] Isaiah 11:6-9, 35:9, 65:25; Exekiel 34:25; Hosea 2:18.

[42] See Genesis 1:29, 9:3; Psalms 23:5, 103:5; 104:14, 15, 111:5; Proverbs 30:8; Matt. 6:11; and other passages.

The forbidding of blood as food was first given after the Flood, and this was greatly emphasized under Law. It is also emphasized under Grace.[43] The reason given under Law was that the blood was for atonement, "for it is the blood that maketh atonement for the soul" (Lev. 17:11). The blood was to be sacrificed, not eaten. This was done, of course, in anticipation of the sacrifice of the blood of Christ. In the Lord's Supper believers drink the Lord's blood only in type or symbol. The symbol of His blood is wine, which in this case, we infer, means unfermented grape juice (oinos: Gk., wine—fermented or unfermented). To drink it fermented would be an abomination because this contains a poison, alcohol. Surely, such a thing cannot possibly be used as a true type of pure and sinless blood of the Christ. To use it is a degrading thing. Nor can it possibly be fit to use as a common drink.

We shall never learn the lesson that God teaches us through the regulation of our foods until we recognize that evil comes to us directly through food and drink. "But of the tree of the knowledge of good and evil, thou shalt not eat of it: for in the day that thou eatest thereof thou shalt surely die." (Gen. 2:17.) "And the eyes of both of them were opened, and they knew that they were naked." (Gen. 3:7.) Man has been paying the penalty of shame ever since the first sin. There has been no escape.

"Ye have not eaten bread (God supplied them manna from heaven instead while they were in the wilderness), neither have ye drunk wine or strong drink: that ye might know that I am the Lord your God." (Deut. 29:6.) This and other passages, when read in their full context, plainly show that obedience in eating and drinking is essential to a true knowledge of God as Lord. In I Timothy 4:3 we read, "Forbidding to marry, and commanding to abstain from meats (foods), which God hath created to be received with thanksgiving of them which believe and know the truth." This passage in its full context shows that abstinence

---

[43] See Gen. 9:4; Lev. 7:26, 27, 19:26; Deut. 12:16-23; Acts 15:20.

170

from the foods that God created for food is not to be sanctioned either. Man cannot take the matter of foods into his own hands and attempt to run ahead of the Creator, because God has ordained what is best under the circumstances. The context here shows that he who does this thing evidences a departure from the faith in the latter times.

Believers are required to avoid giving offense by their eating and drinking. "That ye abstain from meats offered to idols, and from blood, and from things strangled, and from fornication: from which if ye keep yourselves, ye shall do well." (Acts 15:29.) "Whether therefore ye eat, or drink or whatsoever ye do, do all to the glory of God. Give none offense, neither to the Jews, nor to the Gentiles, nor to the church of God." (I Cor. 10:31, 32.)

Tobacco is a plant that contains one of the deadliest poisons. No animal will eat tobacco. Man alone chews, snuffs, and smokes it. This is one of the very greatest perversions of nature. The habit stands condemned from every standpoint.

VI. Scriptures Often Misinterpreted

License, miscalled liberty under Grace, is often defended by misquoting or misinterpreting Scriptures. Some of the most common examples of this are the following:

(1) "Whatsoever thing from without entereth into the man, it cannot defile him" (Mark 7:18, 19.) In the passage in which this verse is found, Jesus is not instructing His disciples to set aside the Dietary Laws of Moses. He is rebuking the Pharisees for overemphasizing the traditions of the elders regarding the eating of bread with unwashed hands; also for holding to the traditions pertaining to the washing of cups, pots, brazen vessels, and tables before eating. Furthermore, they were teaching for authoritative doctrines the commandments of men (v.7) at the expense of God's commandments (vv. 8, 9, and 13). What Jesus set aside was the tradition of the elders, not the Dietary Laws of

Moses. Jesus emphasized the Law. Indeed, verses 9-13 of this very passage show this emphasis.

(2) "I know, and am persuaded by the Lord Jesus, that there is nothing unclean of itself: but to him that esteemeth any thing to be unclean, to him it is unclean." (Rom. 14:14.) "All things indeed are pure; but it is evil for that man who eateth with offense." (v. 20.) The subject under consideration pertains to the Christian's attitude toward others who indulge in doubtful habits in matters of eating and other things about which there is variance of opinion. The foods which were expressly forbidden by the Law of Moses cannot, in the very nature of the case, be considered <u>doubtful</u> things. The things of God's Law are definite, not doubtful.

(3) "And saw heaven opened, and a certain vessel descending unto him, as it had been a great sheet knit at the four corners, and let down to the earth. Wherein were all manner of four-footed beasts of the earth, and wild beasts, and creeping things, and fowls of the air. And there came a voice unto him, Rise, Peter; kill, and eat." (Acts 10:11-13.) Peter refused to eat because of the Laws of Moses, under which he as a Jew had been brought up. The voice did not condemn him for refusing to eat; it merely said, "What God hath cleansed, that call not thou common" (v. 15). Thus Peter was not now commanded to eat of the animals let down from heaven; he was merely told not to call what God hath cleansed common. And all were drawn up again into heaven (v. 16), making it impossible for Peter to eat them.

In verse 28 we have the record of Peter's testimony concerning the matter. He said, "God hath showed me that I should not call any <u>man</u> common or unclean."

(4) "If any of them that believe not bid you to a feast, and ye be disposed to go; whatsoever is set before you, eat, asking no question for conscience sake." (I Cor. 10:27.) This could not be taken as authority for setting aside the Dietary Laws of Moses, for this would offend the Jews. Nor is there any permission given to offend the Gentile, nor the church of God. "It is good

neither to eat flesh, nor to drink wine, nor any thing whereby thy brother stumbleth, or is offended, or is made weak (Rom. 14:21.)

(5) "Whatsoever is set before you, eat, asking no question for conscience sake." The disobedient will seek to justify their disregard of food restrictions under Law on the ground that under Grace, they may avail themselves of this Scripture. At the same time, they will insist on exemption from the requirement of not giving offense. They want the authority of the Word only when it suits them according to their own interpretation.

(6) "Forbidding to marry, and commanding to abstain from meats (foods), which God hath created to be received with thanksgiving of them which believe and know the truth. For every creature of God is good, and nothing to be refused, if it be received with thanksgiving: for it is sanctified by the word of God and prayer." (I Tim. 4:3-5.)

The reason sometimes given by Christians for not refusing the foods which were condemned by Moses is that "every creature of God is good." This could not possibly mean the animals pronounced unclean under the Law of Moses. God did not create unclean and defiled animals in such a condition. As they are found today, they are the creatures of sin. Only a heathen or a greatly misled believer would want to disobey God by using such forbidden food. Yet there are those who assert that this Scripture justifies the eating of anything if it is sanctified by prayer.

This is a perversion of what the passage states. The word here translated "meats" does not mean animal flesh, but <u>food in general</u>. These "meats", or foods, which God created for this purpose could include only such as were given before man's sin, as named in Gen. 1:29.

The passage is a prophecy pertaining to the latter days and refers to those who would do away with all animal flesh as food. That is strongly condemned (vv. 1-3).

False standards regarding marriage are always condemned in the Bible. The fact that such condemnation is found here in the same context with the condemnation concerning foods remind one of the relationship between wrong eating and wrong social relations. We are at the present time living in the fulfillment of this prophecy also. Witness the nudist societies that have sprung up, also the laxness regarding marriage and divorce.

(7) "Let no <u>man</u> therefore judge you in meat, or in drink, or in respect of an holyday, or of the new moon, or of the Sabbath days." (Col. 2:16.) The thing that is set aside here is not the Dietary Laws of Moses, which are a part of the Word of God, but the ways of <u>man</u>, which are the ways of the world. Thus the Bible is upheld as consistent and accurate.

Having considered the principle Scriptures that are often misinterpreted by those who are misled or who seek to justify themselves falsely on Scriptural ground, we do not find a single justification for changing the Dietary Laws of Moses or for setting them aside under Grace.

The reason for this is not difficult to find. Under the dispensation of the Law, the chosen people were required to live a holy and a separated life in <u>anticipation</u> of the coming of the Son of Man in the flesh; under Grace, the chosen people are expected to live the separated and holy life in <u>realization</u> of His having come in the flesh, and in the blessed hope of His future Second Coming.[44] "Wherefore come out from among them, and be ye separate, saith the Lord, and touch not the unclean thing. . . . For ye are bought with a price; therefore glorify God in your body, and in your spirit, which are God's." (II Cor. 6:17 ; I Cor. 6:20.)

Let us cite a single illustration of the difference in standards under Law and Grace. In Israel polygamy was very common and was permitted. Under Grace, monogamy is strictly required. The requirements for chastity also were raised. "Ye have heard that it was said by them of old time, Thou shalt not commit adultery: But I say unto you, That whosoever looketh upon a

---

[44] Titus 2:11-14; and I Thes. 5:23.

woman to lust after her hath committed adultery with her already in his heart." (Matt. 5:27, 28.)

These spiritual requirements under Grace as compared with those under Law leave no room for doubt regarding our duty in maintaining the standards of diet given under Law, instead of lowering them. The higher the spiritual standards are, the higher food standards must be in order to support them. Living the separated life requires that we follow God's direction instead of following the customs of the disobedient world. The requirement extends to all foods on which God has expressed His will.

We are not at liberty to choose our food according to our own tastes and whims in disregard of God's requirements. Nor are we at liberty to follow the customs of the world in order to avoid criticism. The faithful Christian has ever to contend against the hostile world.

The most important thing which God requires is obedience. Obedience is rare in this increasingly lawless age. The first sin was an act of disobedience in eating. Much of the sin in the days before the Flood, we infer from Matthew 24:38, 39, was connected with eating and drinking. Disobedience in matters pertaining to eating and drinking now is, we believe, an important cause of the Age of Lawlessness. Grace abused becomes license and this soon leads to defiant lawlessness. Grace too long abused compels judgment as its only remedy.

An enlightening passage of Scripture on so-called liberty under Grace is the following: "What then? shall we sin, because we are not under law, but under grace? God forbid. Know ye not, that to whom ye yield yourselves servants to obey, his servants ye are to whom ye obey; whether of sin unto death, or of obedience unto righteousness? But God be thanked, that ye were the servants of sin, but ye have obeyed from the heart that form of doctrine which was delivered unto you. Being then made free from sin, ye became the servants of righteousness." (Rom. 6:15-18.) This makes it plain that we become the servants of what we serve. When we escape the Law by turning to Grace,

175

the latter becomes our master in righteousness. Hence, we are its servants. This requires full obedience (Matt. 5:48). This can never be realized through disobedience in eating.

How can we be justified in eating the flesh of unclean animals, when they were strictly forbidden for sacrifice? (See Gen. 8:20; Lev. 22:19; Deut. 17:1; and other passages.) A thing not fit to offer before God in sacrifice, is most certainly not a fit thing to maintain the health and strength of the temple of God, which is the human body. A sacrifice counted an abomination is equally abominable as a food (Isa. 65:4).

In closing this subject, we should not fail to observe that food is for the strength of the body directly. It also affects the spirit indirectly. It appears that natural food is meant as a type of the food for the spirit. This is plainly taught in giving the Israelites manna (Ex. 16: 14-17). It was physical food used as the type of Christ (John 6:27-35). We are especially told that if we would live forever, we must have the "bread of life," which is Christ Himself. Physical bread, or food alone, leads to physical death finally (Matt. 4:4; Luke 4:4) in our present world of sin. Before man sinned this was not the case.

The depravity of sin has greatly degraded not only cultural standards, but also the appetites for food as well. Savagery is a result of this very thing. An examination of the food of the race as a whole reveals the fact that there are some who eat almost anything. There are people who eat every filthy thing, from snails and worms to snakes. Those who eat the most defiled and vilest foods die the earliest and lead the least useful lives. They are the ones who are the farthest from God and are the most in need of help. The Gospel is carried to them by missionaries, though all have not yet been reached.

Under the Age of Grace there has been so much departure from Biblical requirements regarding food that it is now almost universally believed that a Christian may eat anything he pleases. The food that God gave to man before his sin was given not in a permissive, but in a positive sense. "To you it shall be for meat." (Gen. 1:29.) After man's first sin, when the herb of the field was

176

added for food, it was also given in a positive way. "Thou shalt eat the herb of the field." (Gen. 3:18.) When the flesh of certain clean animals was added under the Laws of Moses, it was also a positive command. "These ye shall eat." (Lev. 11:2.)

Sinful man takes the gift of food from God usually without recognizing the giver. He takes also what is forbidden; Eve was the first to do this. Her act was a serious sin. Let us as Christians examine ourselves for acts of similar disobedience.

VII. Food in the Millennium

The food requirement in the coming Millennial dispensation is not stated in the Bible except by inference. We make our inference from what God has done in the past. Sin will not be fully done away with until after the close of the Millennium. We know this from the prediction of a great rebellion at its close (Rev. 20:8, 9). God's Word cannot change. The food given to man in Genesis 1:29 was for him in the sinless condition. The foods given in each subsequent dispensation were for man in his state of sin at the time the foods were given. It seems that in the Millennium food requirements will be gradually restored as sin disappears. It will be in keeping with the principles sanctioned during the former dispensations.

Summary

In summarizing the subject of food as given in the Bible, we observe that no food given to man in one dispensation was ever withdrawn later. No food expressly forbidden in one dispensation was ever sanctioned in a later dispensation. This is in keeping with the fact that God's Word does not change. A food forbidden because of being unclean must remain forbidden as long as it continues unclean. Since its uncleanness is due to sin, it must continue as long as the world is under the curse.

Grain and fruit were the original food given before man's sin, and this food has never been withdrawn. Although man by

177

his sin forfeited his right to this food, yet it has been given to him anyway as an act of love and mercy. Through all the generations of sin this class of food has been the chief one for mankind of every clime and age.

The animals that have fallen under the influence of sin to the greatest extenet are those of the carnivorous and scavenger class. These animals were all emphatically forbidden as sacrifices and also as food. The animals given for food are those that have come under the influence of sin to the least degree. These are still herbivorous.

All of our food is given us as the type of Christ, the Bread of Life. It is evident then that no food defiled through sin could possibly serve as a type of Christ.

In the Bible nothing forbidden as food is ever forbidden arbitrarily. There is a sufficient reason in every case. The forbidden foods are all harmful to all people. Indulgence in them is perilous to health.

XVI

THE BASIS OF SCIENCE SUMMARIZED

Special Creation

The Bible begins with a record of the special creation of a perfect world, a world which had no marks of sin or other imperfection. It was like its Creator. Such a primal world is understandable because it resulted from an adequate cause, the Creator. Any attempt to add details of unfinished stages not recorded in the Bible detracts from the Creator and reduces Him to a being of human attributes. Primal creation was, of necessity, miraculous and instantaneous; no other method of creation in a sinless world is consistent with God's attributes as revealed in His Word. It is, in fact, the only method of creation that is understandable from any viewpoint.

Prehistoric Time

The Scriptures mention sin and its consequences. In every mention of sin, however, an adequate evil cause for the result is stated. It is all understandable because it is true to experience. The consequence of sin in the world before the time of man is the first thing mentioned after the account of primal creation (Gen. 1:2).

During the past century an attempt has been made in geology to subdivide and classify prehistoric time. The time-table of geology, however, is based entirely on evolution, a mere speculation. Evolution has never been established; nor can it ever be established in a world of law and order. Hence, there is no possibility of establishing a time-table based upon evolution.

The problem then is to determine whether on reliable evidence it shall ever be possible to establish a time-table in

179

geology. The facts indicate clearly that prehistoric time extended over an inconceivably long period. No one, however, has ever found a reliable way of dividing it into smaller periods. Nor is such a division of time revealed in the Bible. There is no reason to expect that this time will ever be divided accurately according to man's standards. It was a time during which man did not even exist; its secrets have been largely withheld from him.

The record that this period has left, as far back as we are able to trace it, is one of imperfection. Both the plants and the animals bear distinct marks of imperfection. None of these imperfections can be accounted for by science. The revelation of the Bible alone gives a clue. In the Bible we learn that the imperfections of plants and of animals during the time of man were caused by his sin. We infer with assurance that the imperfections in prehistoric time were also caused by sin. The one sin mentioned in the Bible before the time of man was that of fallen angels; herein, we assume, lies the cause of the imperfections.

This subject lies beyond the scope of science; indeed much of it lies beyond the field of theology also. The Bible states but little about it. We must be satisfied, therefore, with the principles involved rather than the details.

The details involved in the life processes during prehistoric times can be inferred only from the fossils found. Obviously, no fossil bed contains all of the life existing at the time it was formed. The fossils found represent only the forms of life destroyed at the time. Furthermore, it is not possible to trace a fossil bed beneath the surface of the ground in order to correlate it with other beds. Hence, it is impossible to determine which forms lived at the same time, and which lived earlier, or later.

The aspects of the problem involving the time relation have been a subject of much speculation as well as dispute. Even if the time relations could all be fully established, what use could be made of the knowledge gained? It would simply be knowledge added for the sake of knowing. The fact of chief importance is the cause of the imperfections of that ancient world. Having determined the cause, which is sin, the next thing which presents itself is of still greater importance: How does it affect man? The conditions of the prehistoric world are of importance only in so far as they furnish a basis for a better understanding of the world of our own time. Even this is of importance mainly as a guide to better living for time and eternity.

An attempt has been made to divide the total span of prehistoric time into six aeons corresponding to the six days of Genesis. Thus the days are held to be aeons. This speculation has no support that is dependable. It is in keeping neither with the inspiration and accuracy of the Bible nor with the language used. Nor with the facts of science.

If the six days were aeons, then sin began in obscurity. Of course, it would have to continue in this manner and to end in obscurity in the distant future. According to this speculation, day and night lose their significance entirely as types of good and evil. The speculation casts doubt on the reality of sin. Good and evil also lose their significance and become mere subjective concepts. All of this foolish speculation has resulted from refusing to accept the Biblical account of miraculous creation by the Omnipotent Creator. It sets aside the power of the Creator and substitutes evolution.

The False Principles of Evolution

Evolution is the so-called method by which higher forms of life or of inanimate matter are said to have arisen from lower forms by natural processes. The evolution of man from animals by any natural process whatsoever is merely one form of evolution. That of the higher animals from lower animals is another form. That of inanimate matter in cosmic form from chaos or other lower state is a third form of evolution. All forms of evolution are alike in principle: The inferior gives rise to its superior by natural process.

181

Any scheme of creation opposed to the Bible is necessarily false because the Bible is the established authority. The Bible needs no apology in order to be understood, but it does require acceptance. This involves repentance from all sin and acceptance of the Savior. In fact it requires full consecration.

As to the principle involved in this, the demands are not different from those of any other subject. The learner of any subject must submit himself humbly before it and accept the facts one at a time as they present themselves. This is true of mathematics, language, electricity, or anything else. The Bible is no exception. Shall the Bible be rejected because it requires obedience to moral law? Or because it demands that the sinner turn to God? What reason shall be given for refusing that which is for one's own highest good? Those who set the Bible aside are both unreasonable and foolish.

Evolution is wholly false in principle. It assumes without the least proof that the lower and inferior form of life gives rise to its superior. This is equivalent to maintaining that an effect can exceed its cause. Insistence upon such a thing is a reflection upon one's integrity.

All points of superiority that the higher form is asserted to have beyond those of the lower have evidently arisen out of nothing, logically speaking. When something comes out of nothing, an act of creation is required. Then, in evolution, logically the lower and inferior is assumed to be the creator of its superior! This is totally absurd. The lower form itself is a creature. Only the Creator has the power to create. Therefore, evolution is counterfeit creation. It exalts the creature at the expense of the Creator. This is paganism (Rom. 1:22, 25). The Bible states that God created all things (Col. 1:16, 17). Hence, the assertion that there is any other way must be false. It comes from the counterfeit god who is the father of lies (John 8:44).

Since true creation is a part of the one and only true religion, anything claiming to be a substitute must be a false religion. This explains why evolution is popular in a world of many false religions. Evolution is really not merely false science; it is false religion.

It is asserted by evolutionists that the primordial world gave rise to life in the beginning and that this primordial world evolved into the world of the present. A primordial mass of lifeless matter that could have given rise to the present system of complex life would be far more wonderful than the system itself. The present system of life only reproduced itself, whereas the primordial mass would be compelled to create life, a thing greater than itself. Creation is an act distinctly higher than reproduction. A cause is necessarily greater than its effect.

The evolutionist professes to believe that the physical world began in a state of chaos before there was life or intelligence of any kind, that life in unicellular form sprang out of nothing and that this lowest form of life produced all of the higher forms including man. In doing this he insists that the effect exceeded its cause at every stage.

Evolutionists admit that their assertions regarding the evolution of higher forms from the lower are not established through observation. They maintain, however, that in an inconceivably long period of time the evolution takes place. This assertion is wholly false because it violates the uniformity of nature and introduces confusion into the world. If this assertion of evolution were true, there would be no distinction between species in any form of life. The end of evolution would be complete intermingling of species in chaotic disorder. The assertion that what is not true under human observation becomes true when spread over a sufficiently long period of time is equivalent to holding that time will change falsehood into truth. It is as if one asserted that the sum of one plus one is two in human experience, but in reality it would be more than two if the process were spread over aeons of time. If this were true, the world would be chaos. In fact, evolution itself is, in reality, chaos.

It contains the deceptions that satisfy the superficial mind for a time. It contains nothing at all that is of enduring satisfaction.

183

Nor is it in any sense consistent with intellectual integrity. For example, it asserts that the world left to run its course as at present will eventually become ideal. The objective evidence is directly contrary to the assertion.

The subtleties of evolution sometimes deceive those who mean to oppose it, and who would take offense at being called evolutionists. Among this number are those who would not concede that the creation of man (Gen. 1:26-28) was anything but an instantaneous miracle. They would hold also that the creation of the animals (Gen. 1:21) was an instantaneous miracle. Yet they profess to believe that the physical world previous to sin was brought into being through stages and processes covering aeons of time. They would have all of this done by the very same God. Their "God" is a miracle-working Creator of the animals and of man, yet he is the god of theistic evolution for the creation of the inanimate world. This is a changing god, a god of confusion and not the God of the Bible. He would require uncounted aeons of time to evolve the physical world which will pass away (Matt. 5:18), and yet only an instant to save a lost soul and make it a new creature that will live forever.

This is not the creation of the Bible. It is theistic evolution. With those who support this view, the gospel of salvation rests upon evolution of the physical world as a foundation. Upon this foundation doubts soon arise regarding special creation as given in Genesis; then follow doubts concerning the remainder of the Bible. Through theistic evolution, modernism has been introduced into the church.

There are also scientists professing to be orthodox in their views of the Bible who take great pride in opposing evolution of every kind, especially organic evolution. They hold to the view that it took God aeons of time to bring forth the physical world in the beginning. They believe also that God finally took six literal days in which to finish a process of creation, which included the creation of all forms of life. Usually they do not commit themselves as to whether it took God a whole day to create the plants, and another whole day to create the animals, and finally, another whole day to create man; or whether only a part of a day was required for each of these asserted processes. Theistic evolution is thus made the foundation upon which opposition to organic evolution is based. This only adds confusion to confusion. It is neither science nor Bible. Strangely enough, many holding such views are evolutionists without intending to be such. Some of the group are so dogmatic as to reject the real truth when they meet it. It is clear that they do not apprehend the essential principles of creation; consequently, they are caught in the snares of theistic evolution without being aware of it.

Theistic evolution assumes that a "God" created the starting material, which was very primitive, and that this later evolved progressively to the higher forms. It is a subtle denial of the God of the Bible and the substitution of a god of speculation. Evolutionists of this kind frustrate the purpose of the one and only true God. In fact, atheists themselves do no greater evil to the cause of true Christianity.

If theistic evolution contained any principle of truth, it would necessarily follow that Jesus of Nazareth, the only perfect man, He who was both God and man, should have married and left a family as the means of evolving man to perfection. The fact that He, as God, chose not to follow such a course condemns theistic evolution completely as false in principle. If evolution were really theistic, it would follow the Bible in which not evolution, but special creation is given as true. If it were really evolution, it would follow natural processes and would be entirely opposed to the Bible. It cannot be both for and against the Bible at the same time. Theistic evolution is a senseless contradiction of terms and a positive evil.

Any rejection of the Bible plan of creation must call for a substitute. There is no escape from this. Hence, there have been numerous hypotheses to account for the origin of the world, apart from the Creator. It is a waste of time to try to consider

185

each one on its merits, for there are no merits. The hypotheses are open to fatal objections. Some of these are the following:

(1). They all begin with matter in some form giving off energy in inconceivable amount, without accounting for the origin of the energy. The universal finding of science is that energy is never created by natural processes. Furthermore, matter itself is a form of energy. Therefore, the matter with which the speculations start is energy. Energy in any form is merely an effect. All effects imply an adequate cause. The cause of the effects assumed is wholly ignored.

(2). The first material with which the speculations begin is necessarily assumed to be in a state of disorder. Out of this, order in an inconceivably high state of perfection is assumed to have arisen long before there was life of any kind in the world. Order requires intelligence as well as power to execute. The speculations assume that the intelligence required to carry out their fanciful plans resided in inanimate material. None of the speculations attempts to show how cosmos can rise out of chaos in a world that has never had life and intelligence in it.

(3). Furthermore, the various hypotheses all fail to recognize any form of intelligence and power to command, except that which is found in the natural world, that of man being the highest of all. Admittedly, no human being would have had the intelligence to design the vast system of things in the natural world. Much less would he have had the necessary power to command its execution. According to the hypotheses, even this insufficient intelligence and power, however, did not appear until aeons after the natural world came into existence.

Thus all of the speculations to account for the origin of the world are worthless. While it is true that the heavenly bodies do show distinct evidence of imperfection, as for example: the surface of the moon, the planetoids between the orbits of Jupiter and Mars, the meteorites, and other similar evidences; it has never been shown that these are stages in the process of developing perfection. To adhere to this would be the height of absurdity, for this view is opposed to established principles of

186

science. Matter running its natural course becomes less and less perfect. These imperfections are stages in the process of decline due to sin. After they have run their course, the whole system will pass away.[45] Any assertion to the contrary is false.

Evolution is popular because it is of man, and many are studying evolution in various fields of speculation in order to keep up to date. They are more engrossed in keeping up with the trend of modern thought than in keeping up with true science.

It is usually possible to trace the elements of partial truth that hold a false speculation together. The thread of truth which has been woven into the false speculation of evolution has been borrowed from special creation. An example of this is the assumption that life independent of any higher power is capable of self-existence and of self-propagation. Another example is variation within the species through heredity, environment, and crossbreeding.

Since life does not originate itself, it is impossible for it to propagate independently of a higher power. As changes take place within the species through heredity, environment, and crossbreeding, while nature is allowed to take its course, there is always decline. Any assertion that there is real progress due to evolution is deceptions.

In order to establish evolution as true, it is necessary to account for the entire plan of things in the natural world on a purely naturalistic basis. Failure to accomplish this at even a single point is sufficient to condemn the entire speculation, for it breaks the chain of reasoning. An examination of the facts involved shows clearly that the chain of evolutionary reasoning breaks at every point when it is tested by true science.

Many sincere ones admit that evolution does not satisfy them. Sometimes they turn to the Bible, but it is not clear to them. They fail to understand because they are not accustomed to reading the Bible objectively on its own merits. They read it

---

[45] Mark 13:31; Hebrews 1:10-12.

subjectively to their confusion. If they turn to theology, they only add to the difficulty.

This is because the creation of the finite world is frequently misunderstood. The difficulty lies in confusing finite creation with eternal creation. Finite creation in the beginning (Gen. 1:1) was complete and perfect, though not eternally perfect. It was brought into being instantaneously, because there was no sin to hinder. Even before sin, time was necessary in order to test free will in finite creatures. After sin entered the world, there was hindrance and delay, because time was necessary to prove the patience and love of God towards His free-will creatures, not that He needed time to do His part, but that they needed it to do their part.

The final creation of the eternal world, "the new heaven and the new earth," is mentioned in the Bible as appearing <u>after</u>, not before, the Millennium. The reason for this is plain. If it could have been brought about any sooner in a manner consistent with divine law and order, God would have done so; for He does not waste time. The eternal world cannot appear until there is no more sin. Since sin belongs to the finite world involving time, it is needful that sin, time, and the finite world all pass away before the eternal world can finally be created. Time is essential to the accomplishment of the great end.

<u>Evidence of Creation in the Sciences</u>

(a) <u>Mathematics</u>

In mathematics we find the most perfectly unified and the most exact of all of the sciences. Mathematics is the oldest, and because of this fact, the most extended opportunity for investigation and for verification of its many relations has been afforded. Furthermore, mathematics is of such a nature as to afford the best opportunity for exact work. Not only are the various branches of mathematics in perfect harmony with each other, but they are all in equal harmony with other sciences.

Man has had the ingenuity to disclose a very great number of the most intricate relations. Much of that which has been worked out seems unbelievable to those not familiar with it.

It is utterly impossible for the system of mathematics to have come by chance. The entire system is a vast array of interrelated laws and principles. All of this is clear evidence of a higher plan, of which mathematics is but a part. Man has not originated a single one of the many laws and principles involved in his study and investigation. He has only disclosed what was already in existence. Yet his limited discoveries all point to the infinite and perfect Power who brought it all into existence. This, therefore, must be the ultimate meaning of mathematics. Discovery that stops before reaching the ultimate falls short of the true goal and proves unsatisfactory. It does not satisfy the deepest longing of man.

(b) Astronomy

The nature of the heavenly bodies, their relation to each other and their movements, are all investigated under what we term the science of astronomy. What we designate astronomy, however, is only our present conception of what is believed to be the truth regarding the subject. The same thing is true of all the other sciences. Because they are human concepts, they cannot be ultimate truth, but are subject to change. New discoveries in the past have repeatedly modified our views. It will be the same in the future. Although astronomy is one of the oldest of the sciences, it is still in an undeveloped state. The chief thing about which there is agreement is the vastness of the subject.

The record of the discoveries in astronomy fills volumes. The new discoveries, however, have not revealed the final explanation. They have only opened up a still larger field for investigation. The human aspect is still as unsatisfactory as ever. The result of discoveries in the subject has been the increase of the number of problems for solution rather than the solving of them. All of the phenomena known to astronomy, however, may

189

readily be reduced to time, space, and energy. All of these are effects calling for a cause.

The astronomer who treats the physical world as merely laboratory material for his science must be superficial indeed. According to his findings, all of the heavenly bodies are in motion at a high velocity. This represents a total kinetic (depending on motion) energy of inconceivable magnitude. The potential energy as it appears to science is still greater. Certainly the sum total of all forms of energy in the physical universe is wholly beyond all human comprehension. In practically every case, the motion of the heavenly bodies is of the greatest precision according to definite law. Even in cases where the motion is irregular, there is a definite cause for it.

Some would insist that the universe is still in process of making; they maintain that matter is being formed through cosmic rays (high frequency radiation impinging on the earth from outer space, neither + nor -). This assertion has never been established. If we should ever be able to make matter out of the energy supplied by cosmic rays, it would be only the transfer of energy from one form to another. It would still remain to discover where the cosmic ray obtains its energy. The cosmic ray is an effect due to a cause. The first cause is quite as necessary for the explanation of this as it is for the explanation of anything else. New discoveries are not to be accepted as explanations just because they are new; to accept them as such is to act upon reasons of sentiment, not of science.

All of the phenomena of the heavenly bodies are merely effects which imply a cause. To the finite mind such a cause must be infinitely great. The God of the Scriptures created it all and causes it to operate according to His perfect plan. Even the laws of the operation of the heavenly bodies are as much God's creation as anything else.

The astronomer, Dimbleby, believed in special creation in the beginning, one which was followed by a reconstruction necessitated by sin. He supported his views by calculations based on facts of the highest scientific order. He used science to exalt God. Unfortunately, his example has not been followed by many others.

(c) Chemistry and Physics

Chemistry and physics are so closely related that for our present purpose they may be considered together. In fact, they were originally treated as a single science. The distinction made between the two subjects is one of convenience in study rather than one to be found in the physical world.

In these sciences no attempt is made to account for the origin of matter; yet this is the basic thing under consideration. Matter as it occurs is subjected to study and investigation in order to bring it more fully under control and to make it more useful. By following this course, physics and chemistry have become two of the best established and most useful of the natural sciences in serving industry.

The discoveries involving forms of radiant energy have multiplied greatly. They have modified our conception of light and have given us many new ideas in related fields, such as ultra-violet light, infrared light, X-rays, cosmic rays, and other forms. Interesting phenomena based on definite laws have been discovered. They are, however, all mere effects. Examples of this are: the effect of light of various colors on the optic nerve, the effect of X-rays on certain mineral crystals manifested as fluorescence, and the X-ray spectrum from the action of X-rays on crystals containing the various elements.

The spectrum effect of the action of X-rays on crystals containing various elements has led to the discovery of the atomic numbers. These numbers are all integral, and there is a different number for each of the different elements. The design revealed in this is one of the remarkable discoveries of the twentieth century. The former distinction between the elements based on atomic weights was fractional and complex. The atomic numbers are integral and simple.

Science has been interested so much in these effects that it has neglected the implied cause. We may well ask, What is the meaning of this remarkable design covering the entire list of elements and whence did it come? The phenomena imply a high order of intelligence that affects all forms of matter, therefore, the entire natural world. Manifestly, it could not have come from inanimate nature; for intelligence must be associated with life as its origin. Nor could it have come from plant, animal, or even human life. None of these forms of life could have originated such a design. Even man does not have the intelligence to design such a remarkably complex thing, much less would he have the power to put it into execution.

Since intelligence must come from life and no form of life of which we have any direct knowledge could account for it, then it must have come from a higher source. The discovery of this source through science is hopeless, because the problem of ultimate origins is beyond the scope of science. It must be revealed to us by the Source Himself if we are ever to know. This brings us face to face with the Creator as He is revealed in His own Word.

The laws pertaining to gases are also evidence of precision in the phenomena involved. To state that a gas expands in direct proportion to its absolute temperature is only to call attention to a fact of nature. Likewise, to state that a gas expands and contracts inversely to the pressure upon it. Back of these laws there must be a cause. Just what is it and what is its origin?

The law of definite composition states that the composition of any known substance in the pure state is always the same. This is further evidence of design in nature. The science of chemistry is entirely dependent upon the reliability of this law. In more than a century since its discovery we have not found the least deviation from it. We are grateful that this is true because of the advantage it is to us in science and industry.

Thus the list of laws discovered regarding the phenomena of chemistry and physics might be extended almost indefinitely. Too often we take credit to ourselves for having discovered these laws and phenomena just as if we had originated them. And too often we treat the matter as if these laws were ours as an absolute possession to put to any use we see fit. We overlook the basic fact that we have produced nothing at all, and that we do not own in the absolute anything that we discover. The discovery gives us possession only of more power. This is also an added responsibility. This fact is usually overlooked. The fact that responsibility carries with it duty is almost completely overlooked.

Man cannot free himself from this responsibility by his mere wish to be free. If one has the right to free himself from responsibility in this manner, then others have the same right and will very soon avail themselves of it. Presently these others will use their power to the destruction of all concerned.

Even the inanimate world was created to function according to the law of righteousness. When the latter ceases to function for a long enough time, a different condition must take its place. The former laws of the dependability of nature no longer hold. To disregard this truth is to disregard the law of true science.

Man has been taking advantage of the dependability of natural law in chemistry and physics to accomplish his own will. This is done largely in the building of labor-saving machinery for the purpose of decreasing the time for labor and increasing the time for pleasure. Man uses his new power, however, to make himself more comfortable in the pleasures of sin instead of using it to serve God. He is assuming without proof that the dependability of natural law as he understands it will always continue. In doing this he disregards the law of justice in a world of sin.

Scientific discovery as a means of making the world better is a failure. The real remedy must be found in a higher power. Here, again, we are brought face to face with God.

(d) <u>Biology</u>

In biology, one of the very first problems is that of understanding life. This calls for a definition of life. Life, however, is incapable of definition because it is a miracle. The unanswered questions in biology from the standpoint of pure science are: What is life? When, where, and how did it originate? What causes it to function? These are questions that no scientist has ever been able to answer. The biologist finds it impossible to say what life is. He finds it also impossible to say why it continues to function. He seldom asks the question, Why should not life that has once begun to function continue to do so permanently? To say, Because it dies, is to beg the question. Why does it die? Surely, not because this is true to experience. There must be a cause back of it all. Life as a system involving parent and offspring is permanent. Why is not the life of the individual also permanent? It is the Bible, not science, that makes this understandable. Death is due to sin.

The fundamentals of biology are found in the Bible only. It states that plants were brought into existence before animals. They were made on the third day; originally, they were created. "By Him were all things created, that are in heaven, and that are in earth." (Col. 1:16.) It states that God created the animals on the fifth day (Gen. 1:21). How plants and animals came under the curse of sin is also stated (Gen. 3:14, 18), the perversion of nature because of sin. These statements are the true foundation of biology, and they make it understandable.

The Bible states further, that when man is restored to his former perfect condition, the curse will be removed from the plants and animals. It is impossible to understand biology apart from this basic fact. A system of life including animals that live at the expense of the life of other animals as at present, or at the expense of the life and comfort of man, is not understandable apart from the Bible.

The animal that is killed by another animal has the same desire to live that all animals have. To state that it is killed because it is weaker is no explanation. The question is, Why should the weaker animal have the same desire to live that the stronger one has, yet not the strength and agility to find a place of safety? Just why should the weaker animal have been created with the desire to live if it was really meant that it should perish?

The Bible alone makes this clear. The animals were created originally to live on plant food. They were all created to live together peaceably. Their present condition was brought about by man's sin. This makes man responsible for it, not God. The view that sin has nothing to do with the present condition of the plants and animals is no explanation at all. It has the effect of encouraging the continuance of sin and misery.

(e) <u>Geology</u>

The custom, as established in chemistry and physics, of not entering into the problem of origins has not been followed in geology. Geology invariably begins with some form of speculation called evolution. Usually, it begins with inorganic evolution in an attempt to account for the origin of the earth and related heavenly bodies. Then it turns to organic evolution, thus vainly trying to account for the origin of life. This custom is followed as if it were essential to science. Much is said about that which is designated "the fact of evolution."

The one who follows the speculation, whether of inorganic or of organic evolution, violates all of the essential principles of true science. Moreover, the trend of the presentation is distinctly atheistic. It is interesting to note, however, that as we draw closer to the 21st century, more scientists are withdrawing from previously held suppositions. Many are embracing the "big-bang" theory. This would seem closer to what might have been, but sooner or later they feel compelled to embrace evolution further on down the line. Not being ever able to account for life, more and more are admitting that they know less than they thought they did. We appreciate their honesty and hope they will look to the true source for all their answers, the Bible.

195

On a mere materialistic basis, it is impossible to understand the origin of the earth, even from the standpoint of special creation. The ultimate truth of creation is wholly spiritual, because God, who brought it into being out of nothing, is a spirit (John 4:24). All intellectual attempts to understand creation have always failed and must continue to fail. The natural mind dwelling in the world of sin is, in its very nature, ignorant of God's ways. (I Cor. 2:14, 3:18-20; Isa. 55:7-9.)

Some of the facts not easily accounted for on the basis of natural law as usually understood are the following:

(1) The highest mountains have been formed last, and the evidence is that they are still rising.
(2) Seismic disturbances with attendant earthquakes have characterized the earth from its earliest history, and yet during the last century they have recurred with increasing frequency and violence.
(3) Volcanic disturbances have increased in violence and frequency in recent times.
(4) There is more land not well suited to the support of plant and animal life at present than there was in the past.
(5) The climate has deteriorated.
(6) The plants and animals of the present are for the most part the dwarf descendants of their ancestors.
(7) The fossils are in the main very definite evidence of great and sudden destruction of life, accomplished mainly by water through flood. They show that the entire land area has been under water.

These evidences of destruction all run counter to the so-called scientific conception that the earth is running a regular course of progress toward a more perfect state. The Bible makes it clear that the earth is subject to the law of sin, and that it has been under this destructive influence since the beginning. As a result it is running down and will finally pass away (II Pet. 3:10-13). Every one of the many facts of geology that cannot be answered satisfactorily through science are easily answered by the principles laid down in the Bible. An analysis of the so-called "fact of evolution" discloses this outstanding fact regarding it: <u>Evolution</u> <u>is</u> <u>false</u>.

The Original Cause

The scientific investigator who aims to be thorough is always confronted with the fact that the true beginning of things is never found in science. No matter what the line of investigation or study, this fact is outstanding. Reference to the original cause is so seldom made that it would almost appear that this phase of investigation had not been noticed. Yet all have felt this outstanding lack.

Neglect of a problem never solves it. It is only natural to want to know where things come from ultimately. Hence, if this phase of any subject is not taken into account in the treatment, we are left unsatisfied. The subject is incomplete, and we feel that our conclusions may be inadequate as we attempt discussion. No final conclusion can be drawn in anything unless we know its remotest origin. Without the true origin of a thing we become uncertain about its history.

A part of radium in the form of one of its compounds manifests energy unbelievably great. A part of the energy is given off as a visible light easily observed in the dark. It is so unusual that it causes wonder. How do we account for it? If we could see the molecules of all forms of matter and their component parts, we should observe a similar unaccountable manifestation of energy of motion. The total energy in the world is so inconceivably vast that even the thought of its origin completely overwhelms us.

The neglect of science in the matter of the original source has become so prominent that the findings of science are being questioned more and more. The greater this neglect, the less authority with which science speaks.

197

It is true that the original source in science is not to be found by scientific means. The desire to know this source, however, remains nevertheless. The Scriptures were used as an authority by the only Sinless Man the world has ever seen. No one who follows His course need fear for his standing.

As scientific investigation has advanced, the number of facts discovered has become so great that no one can fathom them. Each years adds its contribution of new discoveries to the list that is already bewildering even to the specialist in the line involved. How utterly impossible to correlate the entire field of science and to reduce it to understandable terms.

As science itself offers us no hope of understanding its field in the world around us, let us seek some other mode of approach to the problem. A survey of the entire field reveals the fact that all science is founded upon three basic components: time, space, and energy. Let us inquire into the nature of these three foundation stones of science.

Time extended indefinitely becomes eternity. It differs from eternity in that it is capable of being measured. Thus time is finite. We think of time in terms of its units of measurement, such as second, minute, hour, day, year, and so forth. Time is derived from eternity by measuring a portion of it. Hence, time is an effect, the effect of measuring a portion of eternity. Time, being finite, must be confined to the finite world which was created. Time is always measured by motion, and motion necessitates matter. Matter, then, is essential to time. Obviously, time had to come into existence with matter. Since it could not have existed before matter was created, it could not have existed in eternity previous to creation.

Space extended indefinitely becomes infinity. It differs from infinity in that it is capable of being measured. Thus, like time, space is finite. We think of space also in terms of its units of measurement, as cubic centimeter, cubic inch, or mile, light year, and so forth. Space is derived from infinity by measuring a portion of it. Therefore, space is also an effect. It is the effect of measuring a portion of infinity.

Energy is the power to do work. In all the field of science, energy is neither created nor destroyed. As energy functions, it dissipates or runs down and will not function again in the same way unless its supply is renewed. The constant expenditure of energy requires a constant renewal of its supply, otherwise it ceases to function. Because the total expenditure of energy in the world is practically infinite, we are led to conclude that its source is inexhaustible or infinite. That energy appears to be functioning at a rate not noticeably diminishing is only because of the magnitude of the scale on which it operates. The portion of infinite energy which is capable of being measured is ordinary or finite energy. We think of this energy in terms of its units of measurement as calorie, candle power, erg, and so forth.

Energy functioning in a definite way in time and space manifests itself as matter. This involved motion. Hence, matter and motion are included in time, space, and energy. Since time, space, and energy are effects, matter and motion derived from these three sources must also be effects.

The universe is composed of matter and other forms of energy functioning in time and space. Therefore, the universe itself is an effect. Since every cause must exceed its effect, what then is this incomprehensible cause greater than all we can observe or know in the finite world? This revelation has been made in the Bible. "In the beginning" includes time. "God created" includes energy. "The heavens and the earth" includes energy, also matter and motion. We see, therefore, what are the foundation stones upon which all science must rest.

All is expressed in a single word. That word is God. Science as well as religion rests upon faith. An adequate faith must rest upon the foundation on which nature itself rests, instead of the superstructure only. Our faith must be placed in the cause, or Creator. Such a faith brings true satisfaction. In joyous praise to Him, it cries:

"Thou art worthy, O Lord, to receive glory and honor and power: for Thou hast created all things, and for Thy pleasure they are and were created." (Rev. 4:11.)

199

BIBLIOGRAPHY

Brown, Walter T., Jr. "In the Beginning . . .". Phoenix: Center for Scientific Creation, 1989.

Brown, Driver, and Briggs. A Hebrew and English Lexicon. Oxford: Clarendon Press, 1906.

Bryan, B.S. "Menstruation and the Judgment on Eve." Essay. Birmingham, AL: Su-Del Publications, 1993.

Criswell Study Bible. Nashville: Thomas Nelson Publishers, 1979.

Dawson, J. W., Sir. The Origin of the World. London: Hodder and Stoughton, 1877.

Dimbleby, John B. The Date of Creation. London: Nister, 1902. All Past Time, 1894.

Higley, L. Allen. Science and Truth. New York: Revell Co., 1940.

Keil and Delitzsch. Biblical Commentary on the Old Testament. Grand Rapids, Mich.: Eerdmans Publ. Co., 1912.

King James Version of the Holy Bible [KJV].

Leupold, H.C. Exposition of Genesis. Grand Rapids: Baker Book House, 1958.

Neal, Valerie. Exploring the Universe with the Hubble Space Telescope. Washington, D.C.: NASA, 1990.

New American Standard Version of the Holy Bible [NASV].

Pulpit Commentary. Ed. H.D.M. Spence and Joseph S. Excell. New York: Funk and Wagnalls Company, 1950.

Siever, Raymond. Earth. San Francisco: W. H. Freeman and Co., 1985.

Watts, J. Wash. A Distinctive Translation of Genesis. Grand Rapids, Mich.: Eerdmans Publ. Co., 1963.

Yates, Kyle M. The Essentials of Biblical Hebrew. New York/London: Harpers & Brothers, 1938.

APPENDIX A

YOM AND OLAM
(Hebrew)

In the account of the Fourth Day (Gen. 1:14-19), the word
<u>day</u> (<u>yom</u>) occurs five times—four times in the singular and
once in the plural. In the first four instances it means the literal
solar day, light as distinguished from the night. In these four
cases the meaning is admittedly literal. It is its use in the fifth
instance (v. 19) that is in question. Since the passage in which
the words occur is all in the same context dealing with one
subject, it clearly follows that the fifth usage of the word must be
literal also, just as the other four preceding it. If it were really
intended that the fifth word (v. 19) should mean aeon, the word
chosen should have been the corresponding Hebrew word <u>olam</u>
having this meaning. The aeon-day speculation requires that in a
context admittedly literal, one out of five usages of the same
word must be figurative, while the other four remain literal.
Also that such figurative use of the word day (Heb., <u>yom</u>) is fully
equivalent to the word aeon (Heb., <u>olam</u>). There is no precedent
whatsoever for this in the entire Bible or in other literature. It
plainly implies that Moses erred in his use of words: that,
whereas he used <u>yom</u> (day), he should have used <u>olam</u> (aeon).
To insist that <u>yom</u> really means aeon is to insist that in the case
of each of the seven days Moses did not mean what he said. As
a matter of fact, when Moses really meant aeons of unmeasured
time he used the word <u>olam</u>, not <u>yom</u>. This is shown in "Even
from everlasting (olam) to everlasting (olam) thou art God."
(Psalm 90:2.) Implication that Moses did not mean what he said
is a serious offense before all who uphold the inspiration and
accuracy of the Bible.

Furthermore, the word <u>day</u>, when used figuratively to denote
a period of time longer than a solar day, is never used to denote
prehistoric time. It is used figuratively to denote only some

202

period within historic time, which is the period of man's existence. It always has a direct bearing on human affairs. Examples of this are the following: "And as it was in the days of Noah, so shall it be also in the days of the Son of man" (Luke 17:26). "To proclaim the acceptable year of the Lord, and the day of vengeance of our God." (Isa. 61:2.) This usage is common also in secular literature. For example, we often speak of the days of Washington, or the days of Cromwell, and so forth. On the other hand, to speak of the Age of Coal Plants, the Age of Fishes, or the Paleozoic Era, as the Day of Coal Plants, or the Day of Fishes, or the Paleozoic Day, would be wholly without precedent, and foolish besides, because these periods of time were all before man existed and, therefore, have nothing to do with human history. The days of Reconstruction Week preceded the time of man's recorded history. It would, therefore,[46] be impossible to designate any of them by the word day in a figurative sense. The literal day is introduced to the world in Genesis. The word used to express it is yom, the only Hebrew word that expresses this meaning.

A passage sometimes quoted to justify the aeon-day interpretation is this: "For a thousand years in Thy sight are but as yesterday when it is past, and as a watch in the night." (Psalm 90:4.) The reasoning used is that since Moses wrote this passage as well as Genesis, he actually defined the meaning of the word and thus makes the matter certain. In the first place, it must be observed that even a thousand years is far too short a time ever to be called an aeon. This passage, like all Scriptures, is to be understood in the light of its context. The context here is certainly not one of definition of the word day. It refers to the patience of God towards His children, as is clear from the last six verses of the Psalm.

---

[46] [Source: L. Allen Higley, Science and Truth (New York: Fleming H. Revell Co., 1940), pp. 182-194.]

Another passage cited to justify the aeon-day of Genesis is: "But, beloved, be not ignorant of this one thing, that one day is with the Lord as a thousand years, and a thousand years as one day." (II Peter 3:8.) This passage, taken from the New Testament, involves the meaning of the word <u>day</u> in Greek, whereas that in Genesis involves the word in the Hebrew language. Here, again, a thousand years is far too short to be called an aeon. The context is not that of definition of the word <u>day</u>, when used figuratively. Nor is it creation, nor reconstruction. The context is general unbelief at the time of the return of the Lord. The reference to creation is from the words of scoffers (vv. 3, 4) and not from the Lord.

If it were permissible according to the whim of any one to interpret the meaning of the word <u>day</u> out of its context in Genesis, then it would be equally permissible to do so in any other passage of the Scriptures. This would lead to confusion and absurdity. For example, imagine Jonah in the whale for a period of three days of a thousand years each!

Such expressions as "God called the light Day, and the darkness He called Night. And evening and morning were the first day" are very clearly reference to a literal day. To assume anything else is to assert definitely that words do not mean what they say. According to the aeon-day interpretation, the assumption is made that "morning" and "evening" refer merely to the beginning and the end of long and indefinite periods or aeons. Then, if the evening and the morning are the <u>beginning</u> and the <u>end</u> of the period, where is the remaining or <u>intervening part</u> of the period to be found? The Scriptures state that the evening and the morning <u>were the day</u>. This statement is made in connection with each of the six days, thus making it clear that the evening and the morning constituted the entire day instead of merely the beginning and the close. Furthermore, if the evening and the morning were the beginning and the end of an aeon, why should it begin with evening instead of morning, for the morning would be the natural beginning of it?

Aeon-day speculators sometimes insist that the seventh day must be an aeon because it does not close with any such expression as "And the evening and the morning were the seventh day." A discussion of this point is given in Chapter XI.

Here let us call attention to another Bible passage: "For He spake in a certain place of the seventh <u>day</u> on this wise, And God did rest the seventh <u>day</u> from all His works." (Heb. 4:4.) This, of course, refers to Genesis 2:2, 3. The word in the original used for <u>day</u> in this reference from Hebrews is the Greek word <u>hemera</u>. This is the only word in Greek to express the literal day. When it is used figuratively it is used to denote a period within the time of human history, just as in Hebrew, English and other languages. <u>Hemera</u> never means a prehistoric age, aeon, or era. The Greek word to express this meaning is <u>aion</u>. This word is used in the same way in English. If the seventh day were an aeon, or prehistoric age, it should be called an <u>aion</u> in Greek in Hebrews 4:4, just as is done in other instances in the New Testament where reference is made to time beyond the scope of history. This is the only way to express it clearly. If the seventh day (yom), really meant an aeon, then it is wrong to designate it by <u>hemera</u> in Greek. To insist that it does mean aeon is to set aside the inspiration and accuracy of the Bible and to open the way for dangerous doctrine. On the other hand, if we regard the Scriptures as accurate, we have here clear proof that the seventh day was literal. The fact that <u>hemera</u> not <u>aion</u> is used here confirms our faith in the inspiration of the Scriptures.

The Hebrew word <u>yom</u>, translated <u>day</u> in the Genesis account of the Seven Days, was understood by all Israel to mean the literal solar day. This is clearly shown by reference to Israelitish literature. Let us see what the Bible states in addition to what has already been quoted.

"Remember the sabbath <u>day</u>, to keep it holy. Six <u>days</u> shalt thou labor, and do all thy work; But the seventh <u>day</u> is the sabbath of the Lord thy God: in it thou shalt not do any work, thou, nor thy son, nor thy daughter, thy manservant, nor thy maidservant, nor thy cattle, nor thy stranger that is within thy gates: for in six days the Lord made heaven and earth, the sea, and all that in them is, and rested the seventh day: wherefore the Lord blessed the sabbath day, and hallowed (consecrated) it." (Ex. 20:8-11.)

In this passage the word day, both in the singular and in the plural, is the same word that is used in Genesis. The passage is the Fourth Commandment. Here the word day occurs six times. As to the literal meaning in the case of the first three of the six usages of the word there can be no question. All, regardless of their views on other matters, are agreed on this.

Regarding the literal meaning of the second three of the six words in question, there can be no question either. These three words are all the same in the original, as are the first three. And all six words are in the same context, that of keeping the Sabbath. Since the first three are literal, the second three must be literal also. If they were not literal, accuracy would demand that an explanation be given, or that another word or expression be used. If expressed by a single word, it should be aeon (Heb., olam). It is not correct to assert that because the word day does sometimes have a figurative meaning, it must have such meaning in this instance, and that here it must really mean an aeon though it does not say so. In about four-fifths of the usages of the word yom it is literal, while only in the remaining one-fifth is its meaning ever figurative. If in this instance it meant anything else than the literal day, there would have to be an explanation to make the unusual meaning clear. It is not permissible to use a double meaning of the same word in the same context where serious thought is to be expressed. In correct usage this rule is never violated except in puns.

Here, then, in the Fourth Commandment is found clear evidence that the seven days of Genesis 1 and 2 are all literal. To assert that while the Israelites understood it this way, they were really mistaken and had to be set right by modern scholarship is to hold that the Scriptures are inaccurate and figurative and do not mean what they state. We should bear in mind that the Commandments were all written by God Himself and given to Moses on Mount Sinai. They were God's direct command to His chosen people, who were to be a blessing to all nations. From this people the Son was to be born in the flesh, and He will some day return to rule the entire world. To assert that for any reason whatsoever there was any mistake in the commands, or that the chosen people misunderstood, is to strike directly at the inspiration of the Scriptures at a most vital point.

Geological evidence shows conclusively that the days were not aeons. As geology deals with long periods of time, it would not be expected that this science should furnish the evidence for so short a period as a literal day. Nor does the biological evidence fully establish the literal day, and for a reason somewhat similar. It is the science of astronomy that clearly establishes the literal day. This is explained briefly under the comment on the fourth day.

A further assertion sometimes made in the attempt to justify the aeon-day speculation is that the word yom is translated time in some passages. Therefore, on this ground it is held that it could mean an aeon. As examples of this the following are given: "And in process of time (Heb., yom), it came to pass, that Cain brought of the fruit of the ground an offering. . . ." (Gen. 4:3), and, "About this time (Heb., yom) Joseph went into the house. . . " (Gen. 39:11.) The time meant in each instance is a short period.

APPENDIX B

MENSTRUATION AND THE JUDGMENT ON EVE

God did not curse Eve nor Adam at the fall. They were redeemable sinners; they were not the originators of sin. Satan had already fallen and was anxious to perpetuate sin in the lives of the new ruler of the earth—man (Isaiah 14:13, 14; Genesis 1:26).

Because he inhabited the serpent and spoke through it in his successful effort to tempt Eve to sin, God did curse the serpent (Gen. 3:15), a creature He had created for good. We find that even in the forthcoming millennial reign of Christ on earth, the serpent will still be eating dust. (Isa. 65:25.)

Satan appears everywhere in Scripture as an irredeemable sinner, his judgment and subsequent discharge as ruler of the earth having already taken place in the cataclysmic flood of Genesis 1:2, when the earth became (<u>hayethah</u>) waste and void because of his iniquity.

Further cursing of him was not necessary, but a prophecy was given concerning the seed of the woman, Christ Jesus, who would bruise his head, affecting his final doom. (Gen. 3:15.)

Judgment was placed on Eve for her disobedience. God had given the first man and woman all they could ever need, want, or desire. They had only one command—to obey, but failed the test. God would have been justified to have ended the human race at that very time. Instead, He cursed the ground (the dust of which the wicked serpent would eat) for Adam's (mankind's) sake (Gen. 3:17) and placed upon him the burden of toil by the sweat of his brow. The earth would bring forth thorns and thistles and his perfect environment would cease.

By the time of Noah's flood, the defiled ground had brought about a shortening of the life span as predicted by God when He told Adam that "in the day that thou eatest (of the tree of the knowledge of good and evil) thereof, thou shalt surely die (dying, thou shalt die)." Unclean animals are first mentioned at the time of this flood.

Unto Eve He said, "I will greatly multiply thy pain (sorrow) and (in particular) thy conception." The root word for the direct object is "pain", but itstsebhon includes "sorrow" as well, in fact, everything that is hard to bear.

It will be noticed that the hendiadys (sorrow and conception) uses the word "conception" in the translation. This is a better rendition than "pregnancy" because it puts it in the particular ("pregnancy" could include anytime in the nine month period of gestation.) It is also the reason the next clause is necessary, "In pain (this form is briefer than the preceding 'pain' and could be translated 'misery' or 'severest anguish') thou shalt bring forth (which includes 'bringing up' also) children." Here then is the termination of pregnancy—parturition.

The question left then is, What could have been meant by pain and sorrow in conception? There is no pain in conception. A woman hardly knows when it is she has [Source: Betty Sue Bryan, "Menstruation and the Judgment on Eve," Essay. (Baton Rouge: Su-Del Publications, 1993.)] actually conceived. As a woman I have to believe that the onset of menstruation is inferred here because a woman cannot conceive until that takes place.

Who has ever met a woman who would say she was glad the day, as a young girl, she began her first menstrual period? There is a solemn, woeful sorrow attached to it that leads her to believe the experience is far beyond anything finite in her young life, over and beyond anything , out of the control of any earthly person. One can hardly describe the great sorrow and grief attached to it when the realization of its regularity and longevity is reluctantly acknowledged, not to mention the discomfort and uncleanness of it all. In fact, that is the way it is referred to in Scripture—"at the time of her uncleanness."[47]

"This punishment is calculated to keep awake in womankind a direct remembrance of the fateful deed of the first mother."[48]

The hendiadys could translate down to "conception sorrow" like the hendiadys "might and main translates to "main strength" (the word 'main' meaning 'violent effort').

Gesenius (The Pulpit Commentary, Vol. 1, p. 66), uses "the sorrow of thy conception" for the hendiadys "sorrow and conception".

All the commentaries I have researched (all written by men) ignore the word "conception" altogether. No comment is made on it. But it is there and must be recognized. Some even go so far as to say that a frequent recurrence of conception is meant by the word "multiply".[49] But it is the sorrow that is multiplied, actually every month for as long as 40 years plus. That is multiplication.

Others put the sorrows with the conditions of total pregnancy.[50]

To "be fruitful and multiply" could not be considered a punishment since it was God's plan for producing the next generation and given before the fall. But the judgment indicates "the distortion of this intimate and holy relationship as a result of sin's entry."[51]

When God speaks, that which is commanded begins to take place immediately. After the judgment concerning the menstruation was spoken by Him, the first family was driven

---

[47] Lev. 15:25-31, 18:19; II Sam. 11:4; Eze. 36:17.

[48] H.C. Leupold, Exposition of Genesis (Grand Rapids: Baker Book House, 1958) p. 171.

[49] Ibid

[50] C.F. Keil and F. Delitzsch, Commentary on the Old Testament, Vol. 1 (Grand Rapids: Eerdmans, 1912), p. 103.

[51] Criswell Study Bible. (Nashville: Thomas Nelson Publishers, 1979), p. 10.

from the garden. Why such haste, one wonders? Surely much could have been done to keep them from the tree of life, the eating of which would have resulted in living forever in a sinful condition. (That was an act of mercy on God's part.)

I believe that a great part of the speed was due to the fact that the uncleanness of the woman was about to take place and that could not be allowed in a perfect place as the garden of Eden. Once outside it tells us that Adam knew Eve and she conceived (Gen. 4:1). She had not been a mother until this time. After God's promise (in the garden after the fall) that in the seed of the woman would Satan be utterly defeated, Adam "called his wife's name Eve; because she was the mother of all living." At this time Eve had no children, so the proper translation for the word "was" is exactly like that of Genesis 1:2 (the same word hayethah is used): she "became" the mother of all living (Gen. 3:20.)

Source: Betty Sue Bryan, "Menstruation and the Judgement on
  Eve." Essay. Birmingham, AL: Su-Del Publications, 1993.

FESTAL
(Isaiah 35)

Seeing as how someday

The desert will blossom as a rose

And the parched land be glad,

The wilderness rejoice

And bloom like the crocus,

All nature will clap its hands

And cease its groaning

When the Glory of Lebanon

And the Splendor of Carmel,

The Rose of Sharon, the Lord Himself

Shall appear to many again,

Victorious, triumphant, risen;

Why shouldn't we, as we worship

On each resurrection day,

Sunday, the Lord's day,

Wear our festal garments,

Laying aside the common,

Informal, slouchy weekday dress

And prepare the way

For His glorious return?

-Betty Sue Bryan
Gold and Silver Award, World of
Poetry, 1990.
International Society of Poets, 1993.
The International Library of Poetry,
1993, Editor's Choice Award.

BETTY SUE BRYAN

Bachelor of Arts in Humanities from Edison State College in
Trenton, NJ, 1989.
Master of Arts in English and Music from Louisiana State
University, 1992.
Author of <u>Monograms</u>, Book of Devotional Poetry, Su-Del
Publications, 1981.

9 780759 604018